ACROSS THE TRACKS

THE

TRACKS

ALVERNE BALL | STACEY ROBINSON

Abrams ComicArts MEGASCOPE, New York

In honor of Heidi Jennifer Burrell, or as her tribe called her, Little Fawn. Let us remember her and all the indigenous people whose land we built our dreams upon.

Special thanks to the Greenwood Community Center

MEGASCOPE Curator: John Jennings
Project Manager: Charles Kochman
Editor: Charlotte Greenbaum
Assistant Editor: Jazmine Joyner
Designer: Kay Petronio
Managing Editor: Mary O'Mara
Production Manager: Alison Gervais
Lettering: Damian Duffy
Colorists: Alex Batchelor, John Jennings,
Anthony Moncada, Solomon Robinson

Cataloging-in-Publication Data has been applied for and may be obtained from the Library of Congress.

ISBN 978-1-4197-5517-0
eISBN 978-1-64700-340-1

Copyright © 2021 Alverne Ball and Stacey Robinson

Printed and bound in China
10 9 8 7 6 5 4 3 2 1

Abrams ComicArts books are available at special discounts when purchased in quantity for premiums and promotions as well as fundraising or educational use. Special editions can also be created to specification. For details, contact specialsales@abramsbooks.com or the address below.

Abrams ComicArts is a registered trademark of Harry N. Abrams, Inc. MEGASCOPE™ is a trademark of John Jennings and Harry N. Abrams, Inc.

ABRAMS The Art of Books
195 Broadway, New York, NY 10007
abramsbooks.com

ABRAMS   ART
MEGASCOPE

MEGASCOPE is dedicated to show-casing speculative and nonfiction works by and about people of color, with a focus on science fiction, fantasy, horror, history, and stories of magical realism. The megascope is a fictional device imagined by W. E. B. Du Bois that can peer through time and space into other realities. This magical invention represents the idea that so much of our collective past has not seen the light of day, and that there is so much history that we have yet to discover. MEGASCOPE will serve as a lens through which we can broaden our view of history, the present, and the future, and as a method by which previously unheard voices can find their way to an ever-growing diverse audience.

PREFACE

Greenwood, or Black Wall Street, has been talked about around Black folks' kitchen tables and front porches for years. But it wasn't until recently, when the greatest racially motivated massacre in this country's history was showcased on HBO's *Watchmen* did the tale, and even the existence of the destruction of Black Wall Street, become a topic of interest for non-Black people. Most viewers had no idea that such a horrendous act of domestic terrorism had ever taken place on U.S. soil.

But for some—like myself—Black Wall Street is a constant reminder. It is always being talked about as if it were Wakanda, or the promise of forty acres and a mule. I guess that's why last year, on the ninety-ninth anniversary, I emailed John Jennings about doing a graphic novel on Greenwood and its history. I would learn later that the very same night, minutes after I'd sent my email, artist Stacey Robinson had also sent John correspondence, expressing the need to do something to memorialize Black Wall Street.

Maybe it was kismet or maybe it was Divine Right, but now more than ever before it feels necessary to shine a light on the people that once lived in Greenwood when Black Wall Street existed in its heyday. Everyone involved in this book had one purpose and that was to showcase the endeavor of African Americans succeeding in the face of adversity as they built up the community of Greenwood.

With this book we hope to replace a missing piece of the puzzle of American history and help facilitate a new narrative about Black Wall Street that will pique people's interest in learning more about our country's lost history.

We Lift everyone's voice and Sing with the idea that we are one in the living embodiment of what this country stands for: that we hold these truths to be self evident that all men are created equal under one nation under God.

Alverne Ball
October 2020
Los Angeles, California

TIMELINE

1828-36 — Trail of Tears

1842 (NOVEMBER) — African Rebellion at the Vann plantation

1847 — Group of African American settlers found the Republic of Liberia

1861 (APRIL) — Civil War, majority of Five Nations support Confederacy

1863-77 — American Reconstruction era

1884-85 — Berlin Conference (Age of Imperialism)

1887 — Dawes Commission

1888 — Ethiopian movement begins

1889 — Oklahoma Land Rush

1896	*Plessy v. Ferguson* (separate but equal doctrine)
1897	Langston University is founded
1898	The Curtis Act (the breakup of tribal governments)
1906	O. W. Gurley founds Greenwood community
1907	Oklahoma attains statehood
1914–18	World War I
1918	Spanish Flu pandemic
1919	Red Summer (acts of white supremacy and terrorism against Black Americans occur in forty U.S. cities and towns)
1921	Tulsa race massacre
2020	*McGirt v. Oklahoma* United States Supreme Court decision

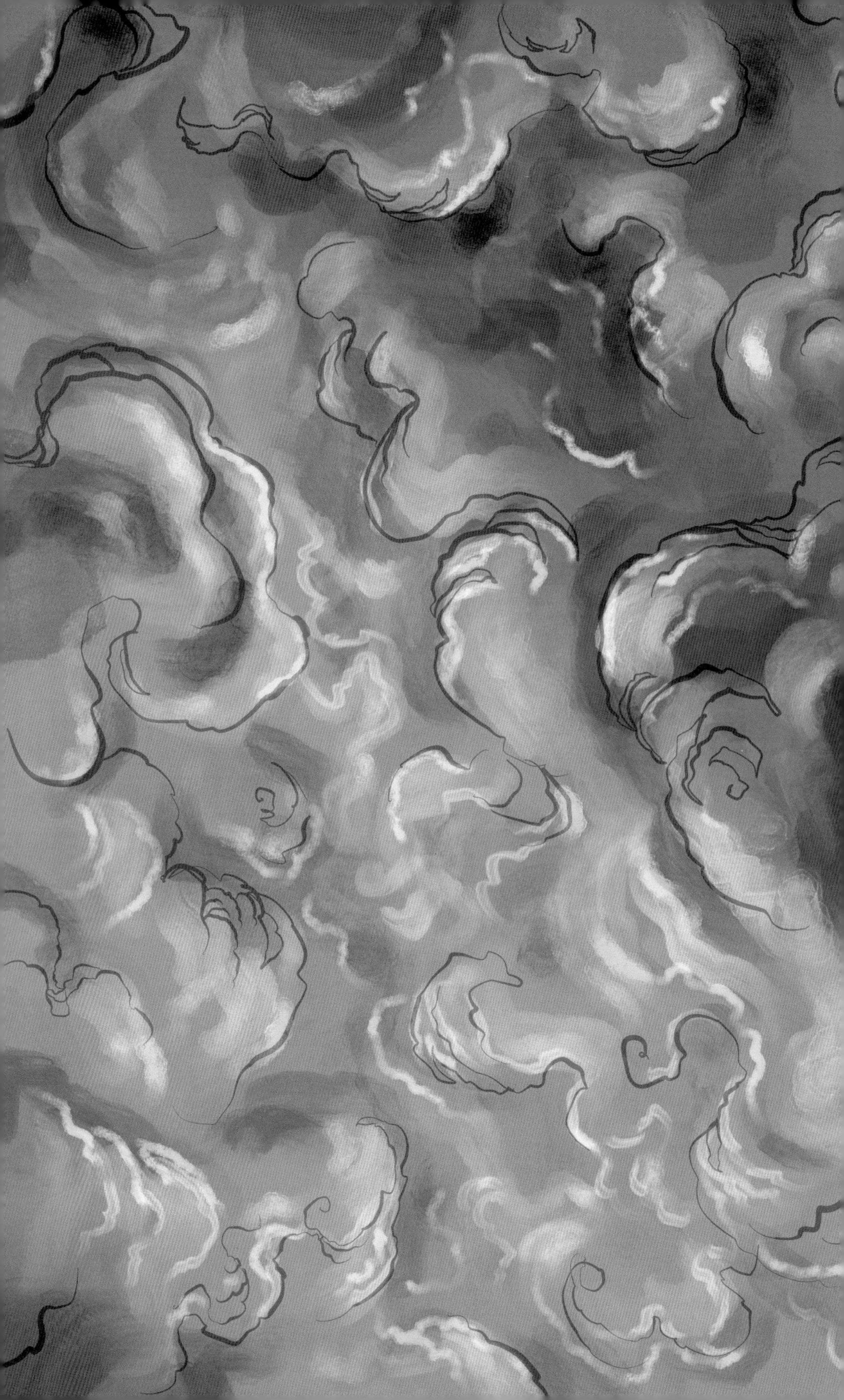

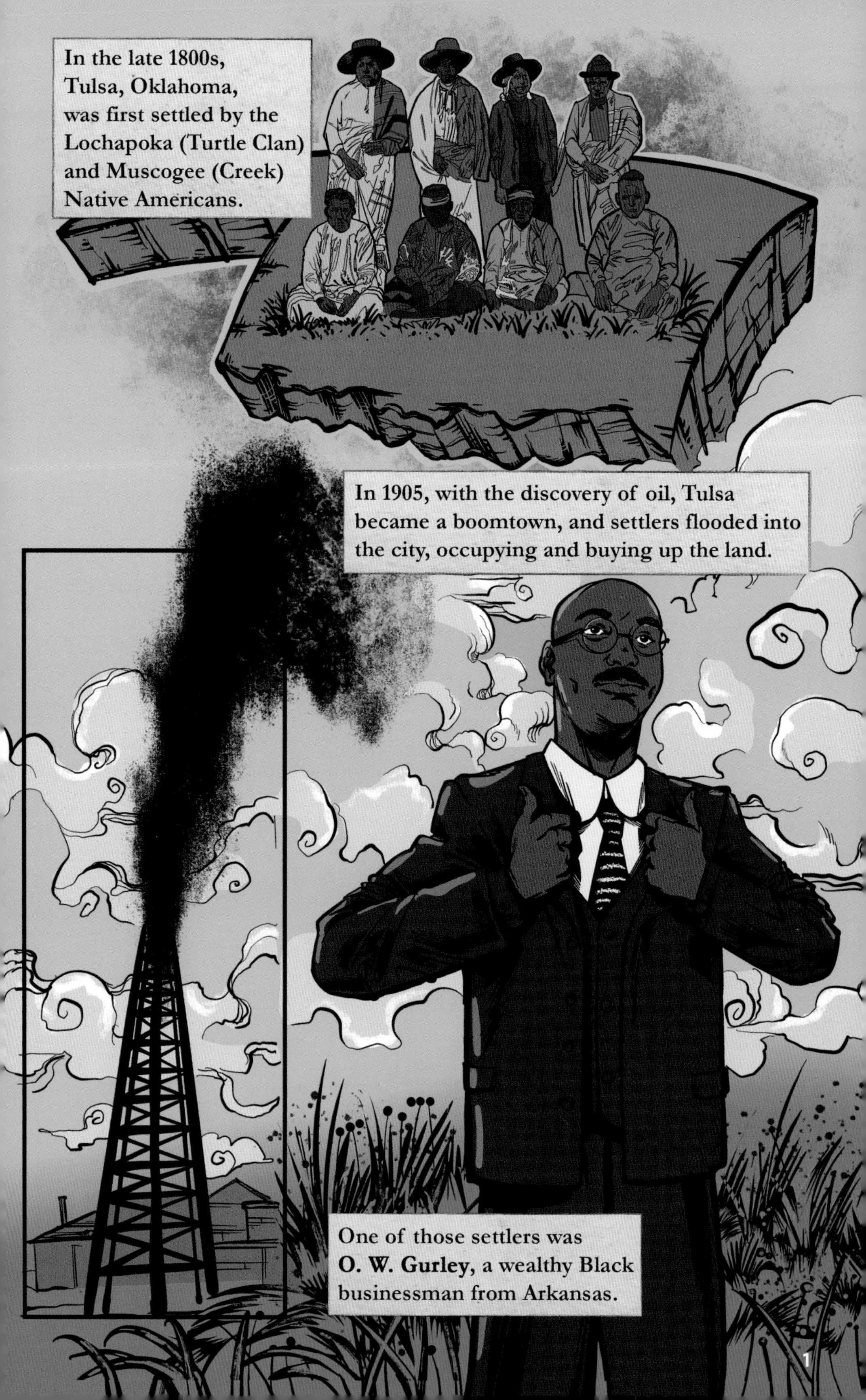
In the late 1800s, Tulsa, Oklahoma, was first settled by the Lochapoka (Turtle Clan) and Muscogee (Creek) Native Americans.
In 1905, with the discovery of oil, Tulsa became a boomtown, and settlers flooded into the city, occupying and buying up the land.
One of those settlers was **O. W. Gurley**, a wealthy Black businessman from Arkansas.

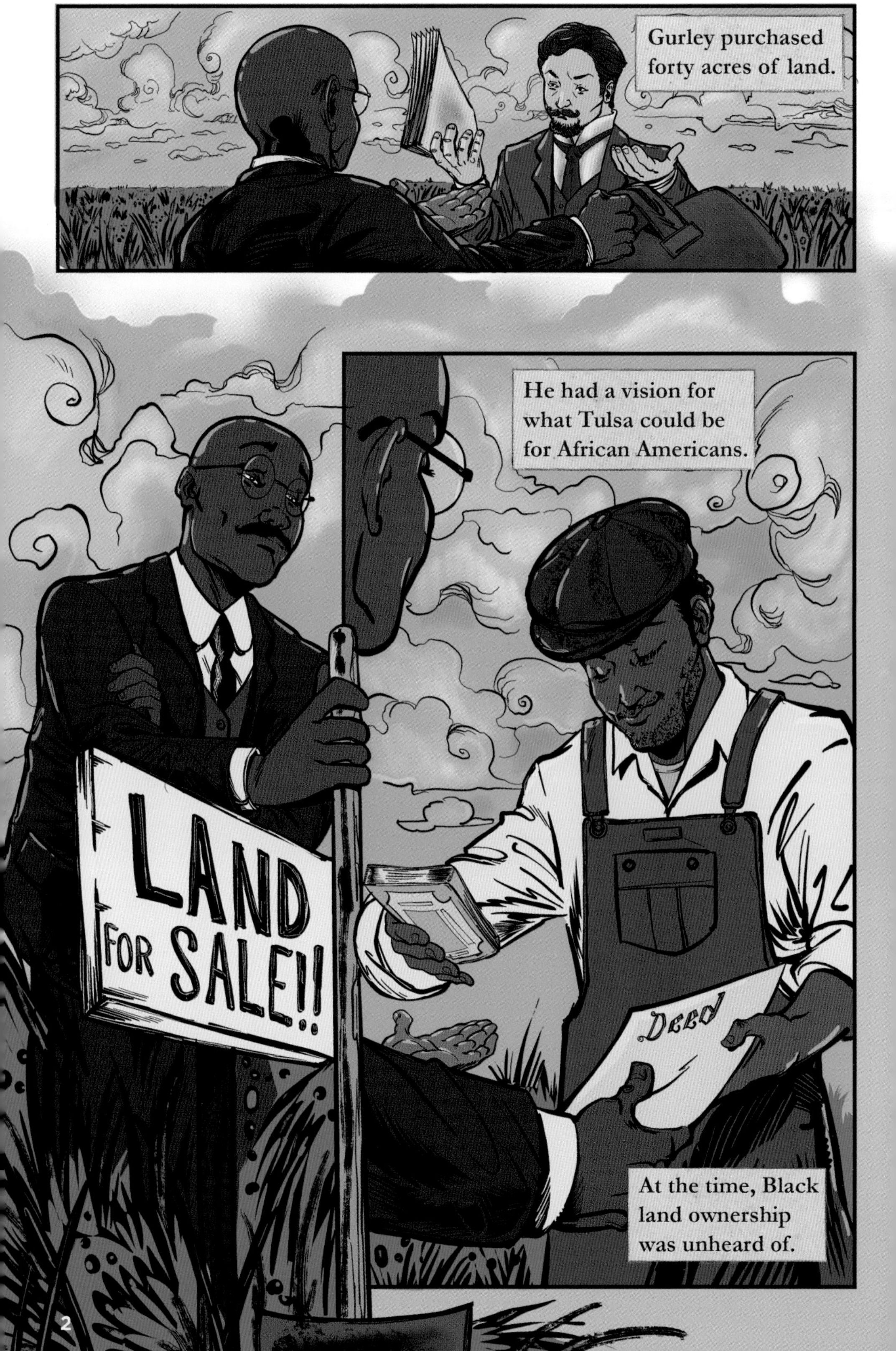
Gurley purchased forty acres of land.
He had a vision for what Tulsa could be for African Americans.
LAND FOR SALE!!
Deed
At the time, Black land ownership was unheard of.

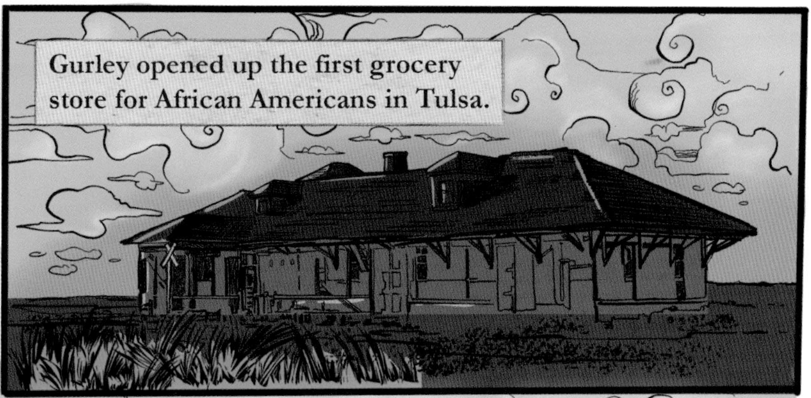
Gurley opened up the first grocery store for African Americans in Tulsa.

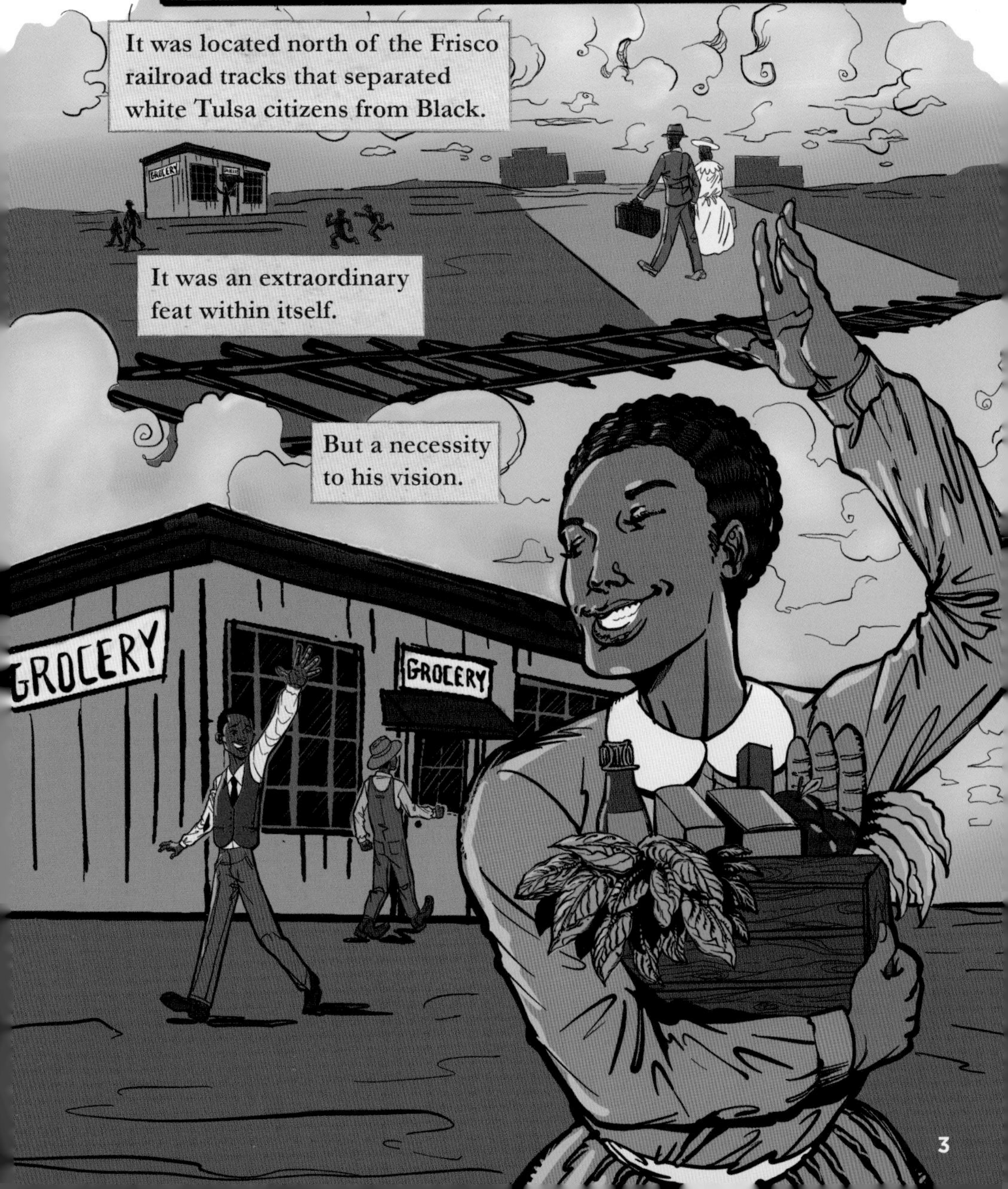
It was located north of the Frisco railroad tracks that separated white Tulsa citizens from Black.
GROCERY
It was an extraordinary feat within itself.
But a necessity to his vision.
GROCERY
GROCERY

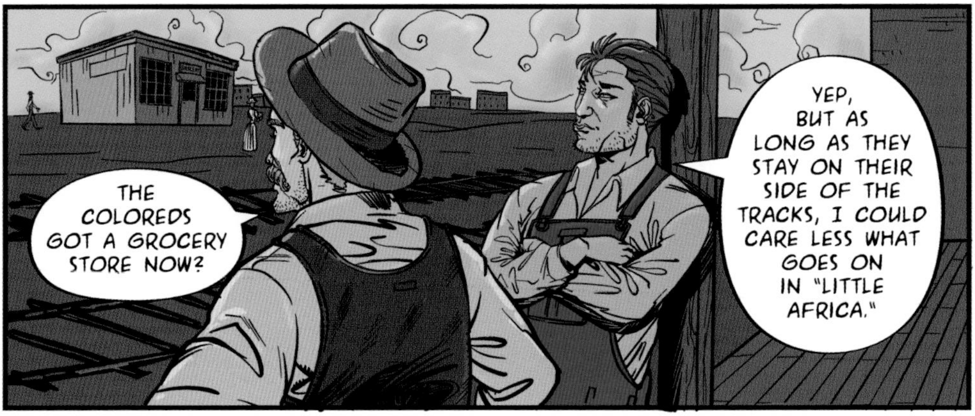
THE COLOREDS GOT A GROCERY STORE NOW?
YEP, BUT AS LONG AS THEY STAY ON THEIR SIDE OF THE TRACKS, I COULD CARE LESS WHAT GOES ON IN "LITTLE AFRICA."

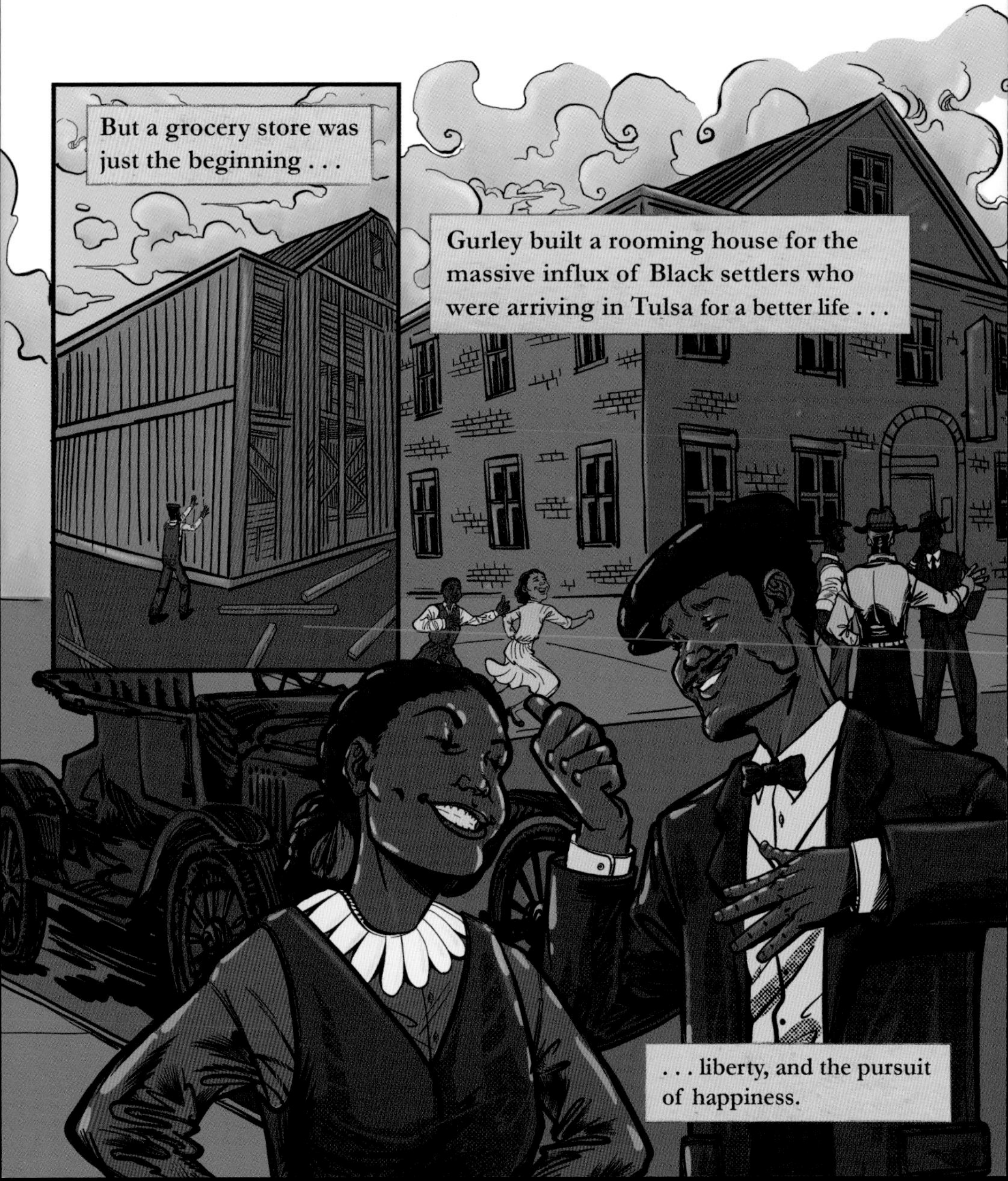
But a grocery store was just the beginning . . .
Gurley built a rooming house for the massive influx of Black settlers who were arriving in Tulsa for a better life . . .
. . . liberty, and the pursuit of happiness.

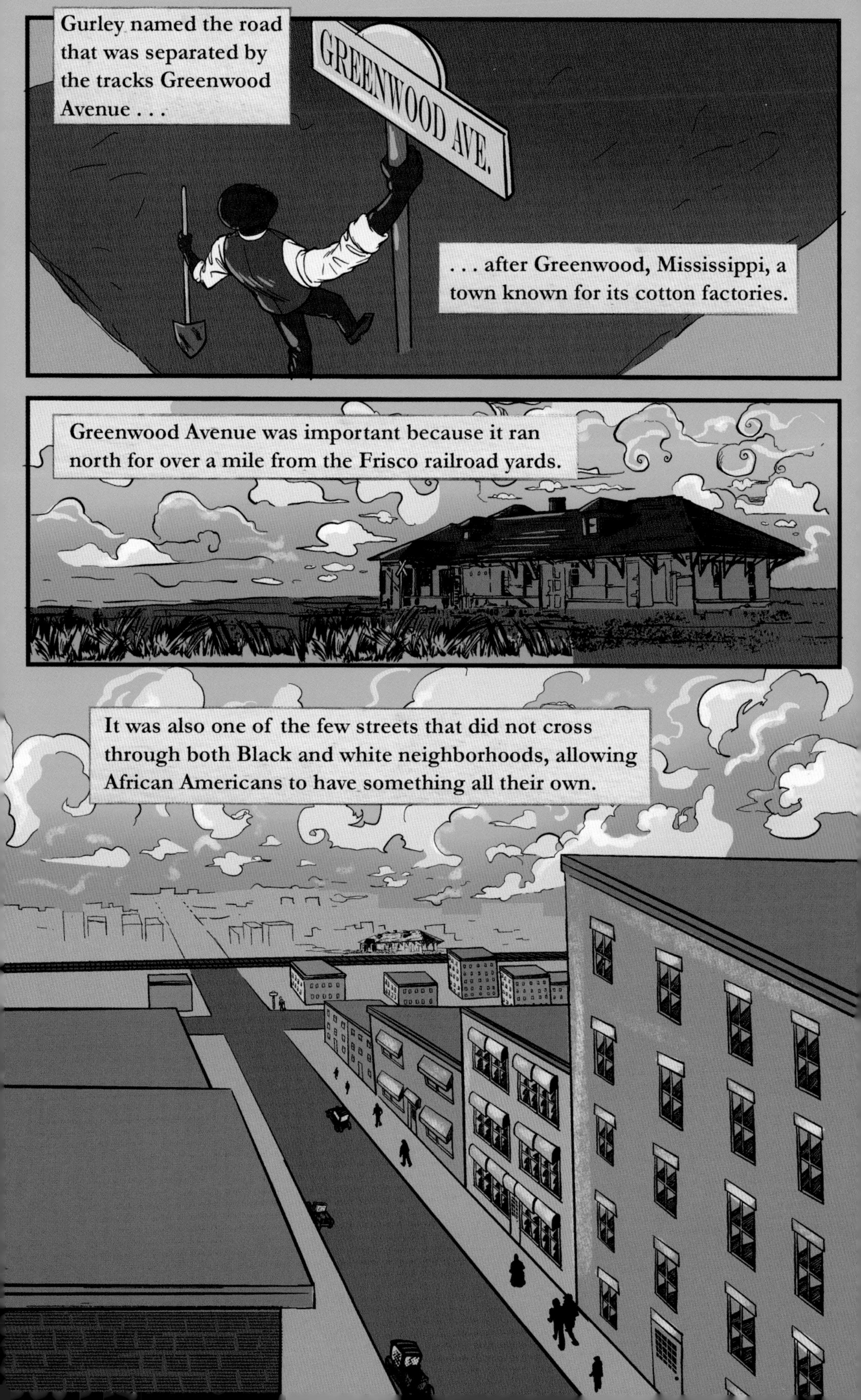
Gurley named the road that was separated by the tracks Greenwood Avenue . . .
GREENWOOD AVE.
. . . after Greenwood, Mississippi, a town known for its cotton factories.
Greenwood Avenue was important because it ran north for over a mile from the Frisco railroad yards.
It was also one of the few streets that did not cross through both Black and white neighborhoods, allowing African Americans to have something all their own.

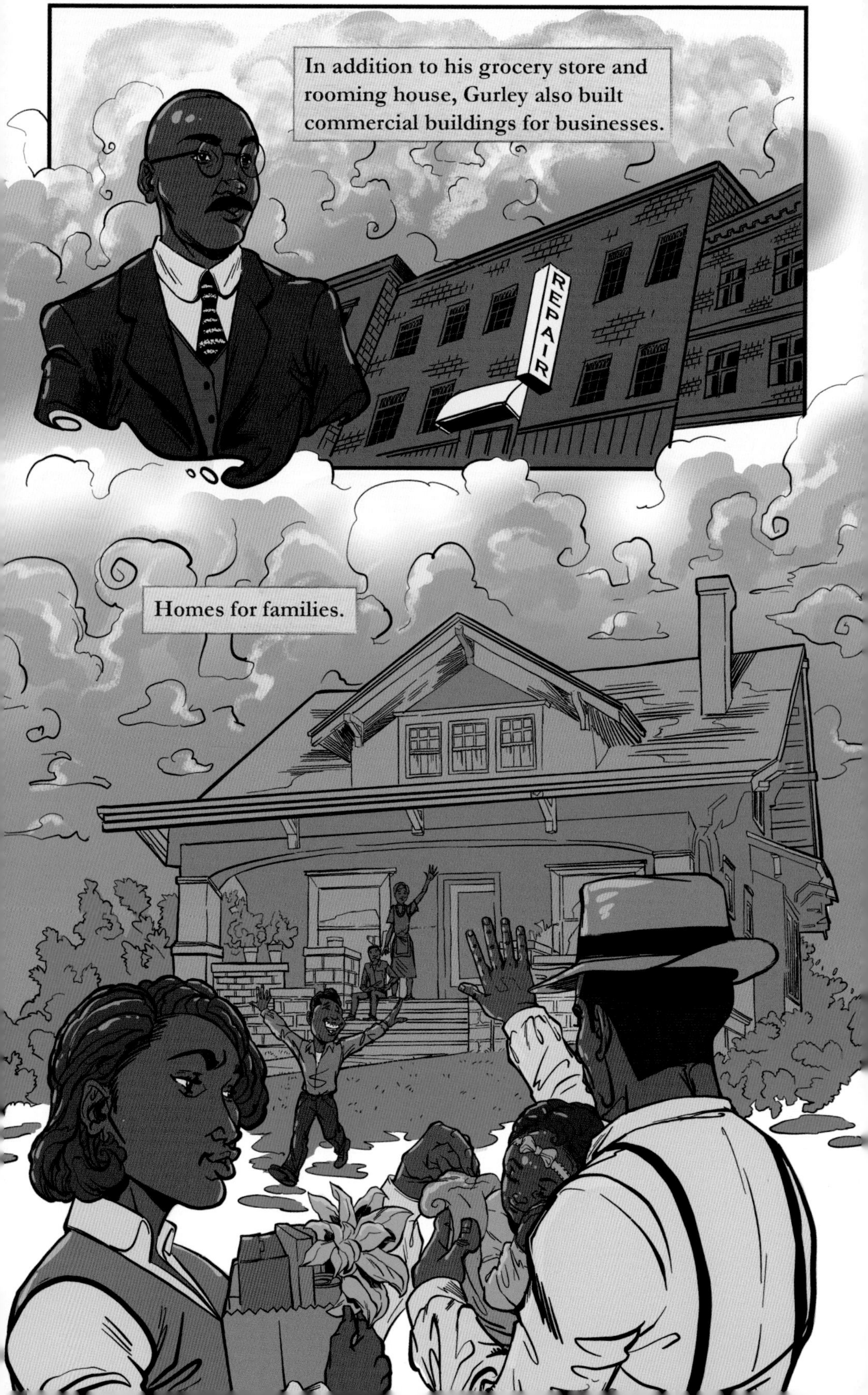
In addition to his grocery store and rooming house, Gurley also built commercial buildings for businesses.
REPAIR
Homes for families.

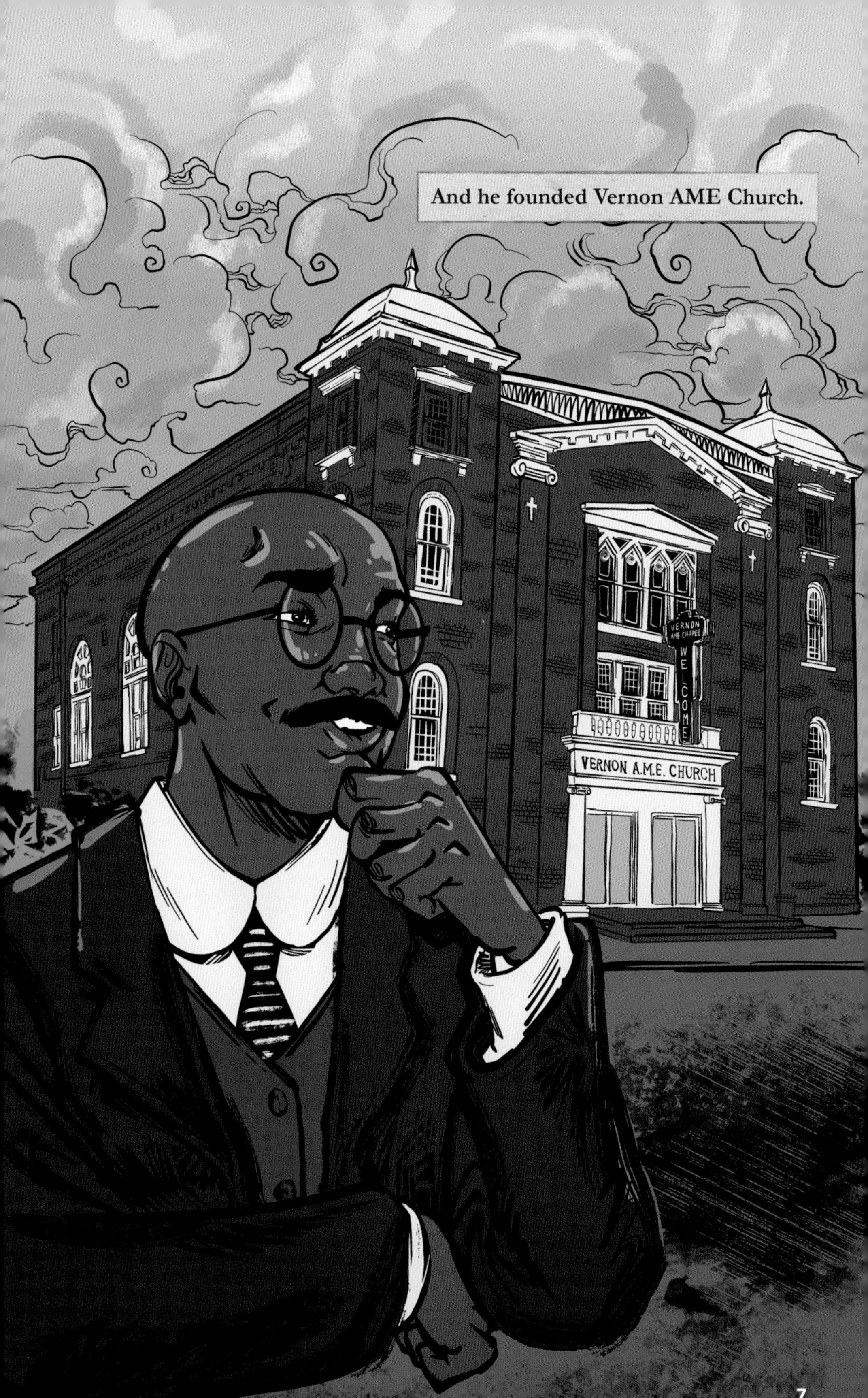
And he founded Vernon AME Church.
VERNON AME CHAPEL
WELCOME
VERNON A.M.E. CHURCH

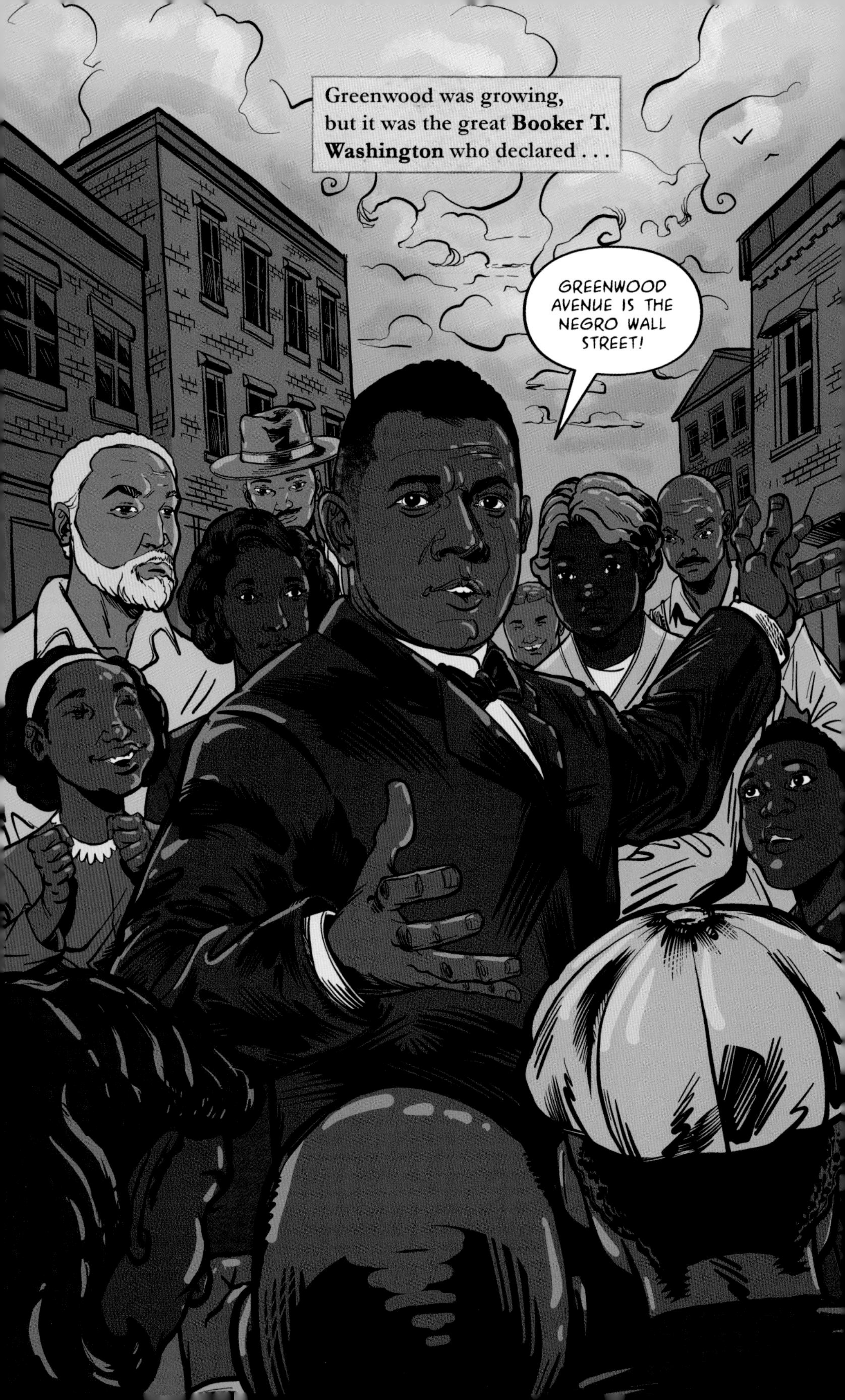
Greenwood was growing, but it was the great **Booker T. Washington** who declared . . .
GREENWOOD AVENUE IS THE NEGRO WALL STREET!

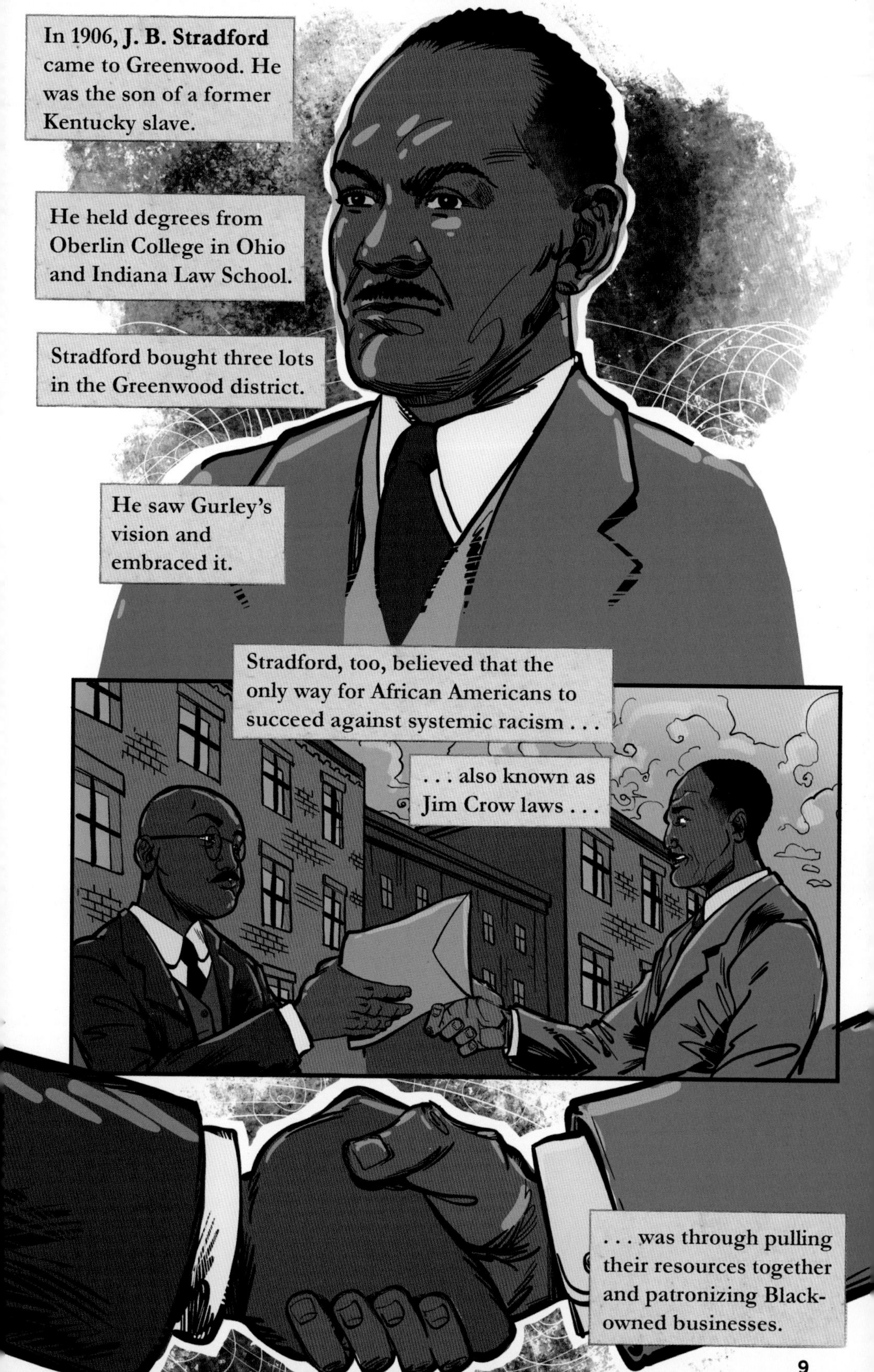
In 1906, J. B. Stradford came to Greenwood. He was the son of a former Kentucky slave.
He held degrees from Oberlin College in Ohio and Indiana Law School.
Stradford bought three lots in the Greenwood district.
He saw Gurley's vision and embraced it.
Stradford, too, believed that the only way for African Americans to succeed against systemic racism . . .
. . . also known as Jim Crow laws . . .
. . . was through pulling their resources together and patronizing Black-owned businesses.

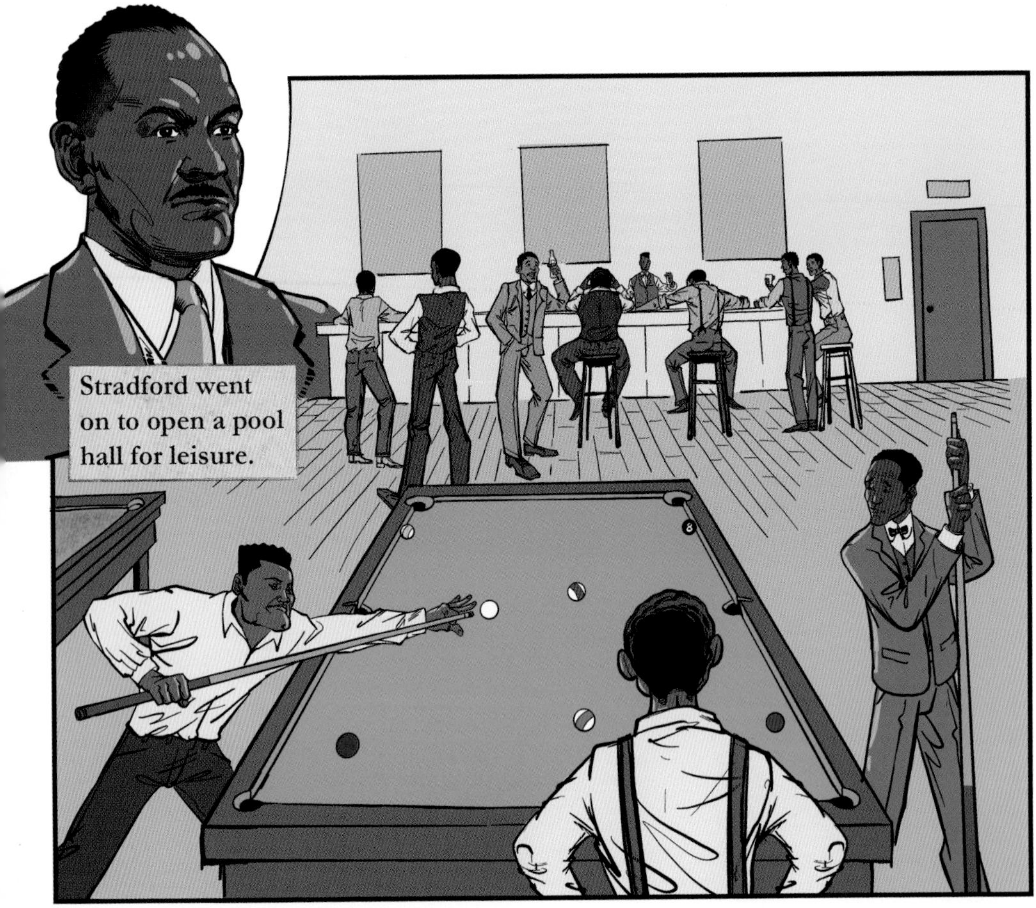
Stradford went on to open a pool hall for leisure.

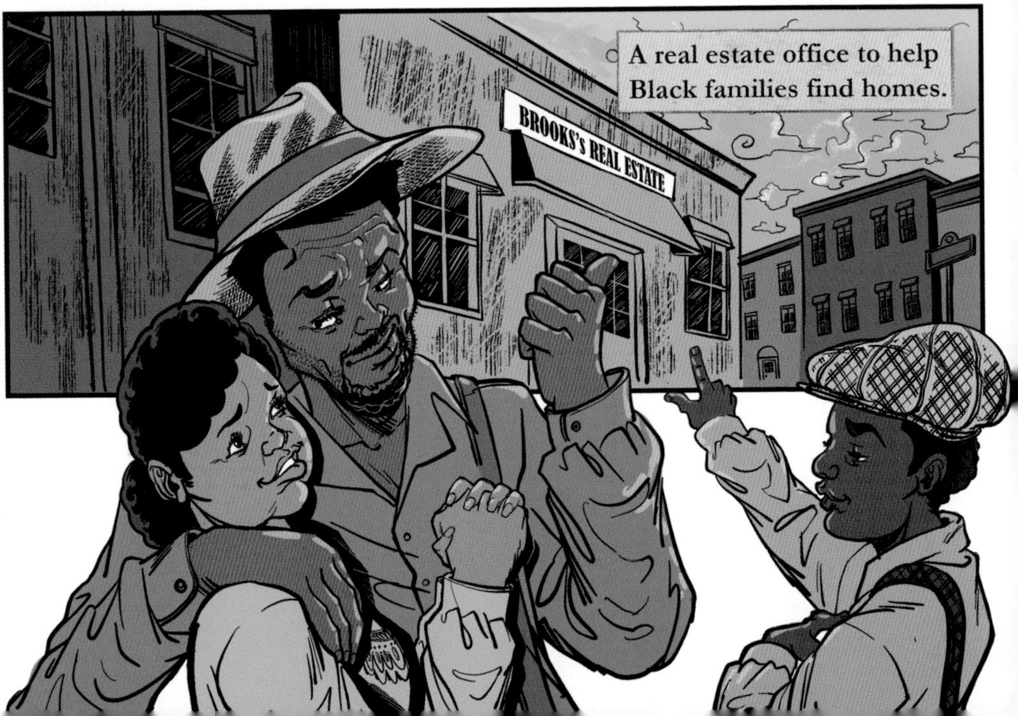
A real estate office to help Black families find homes.
BROOKS's REAL ESTATE

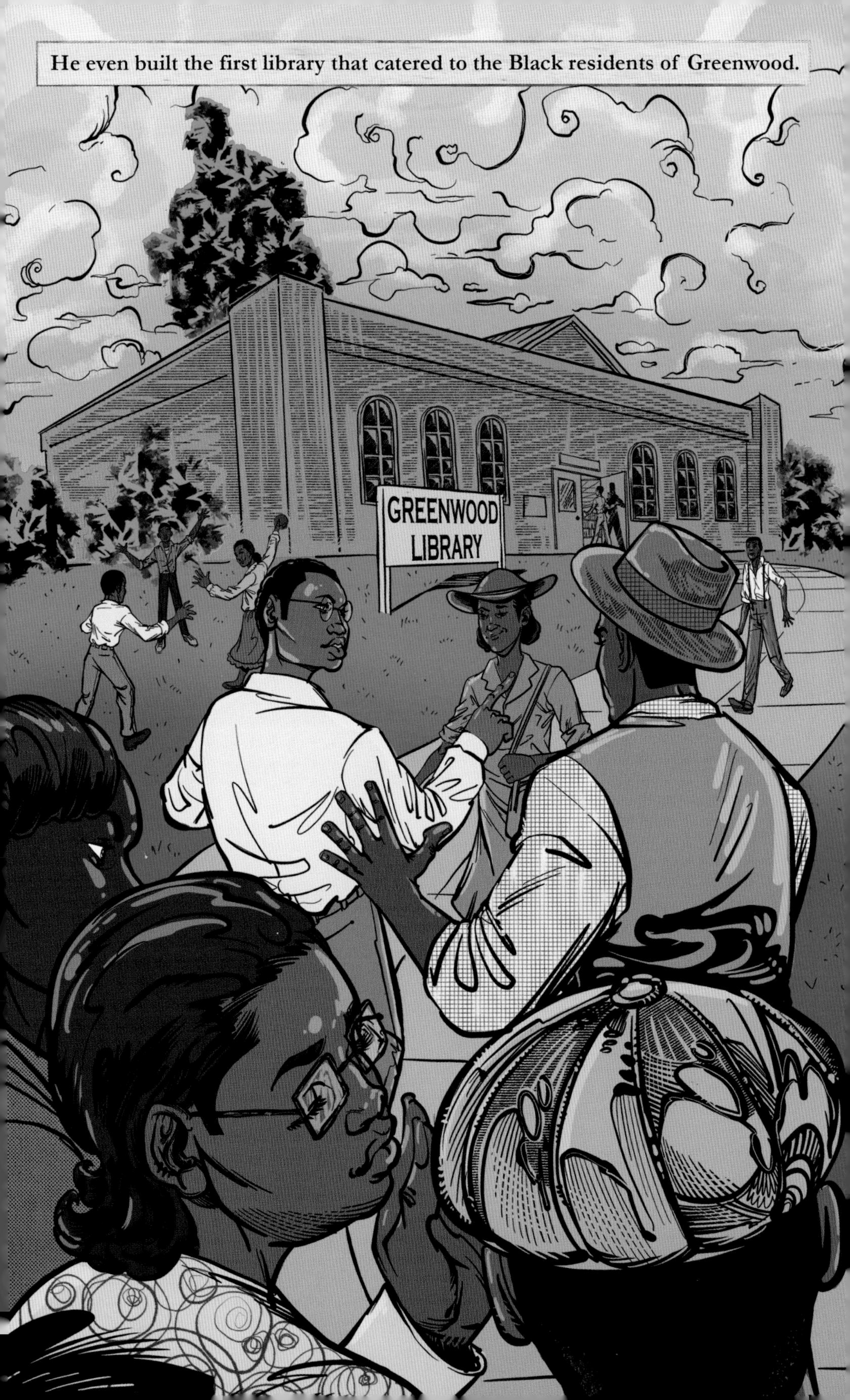

He even built the first library that catered to the Black residents of Greenwood.
GREENWOOD LIBRARY

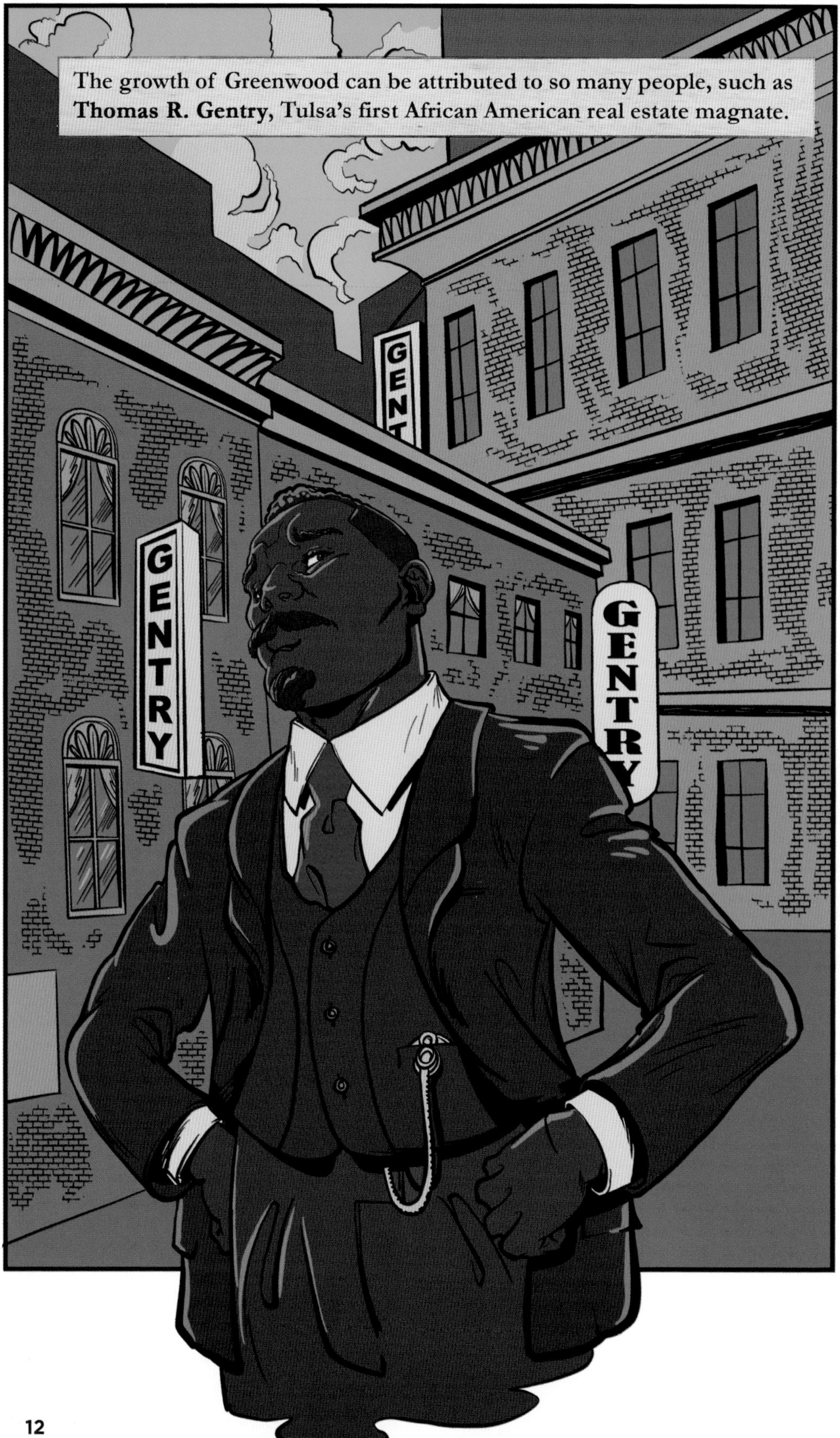
The growth of Greenwood can be attributed to so many people, such as **Thomas R. Gentry,** Tulsa's first African American real estate magnate.
GENTRY
GENTRY

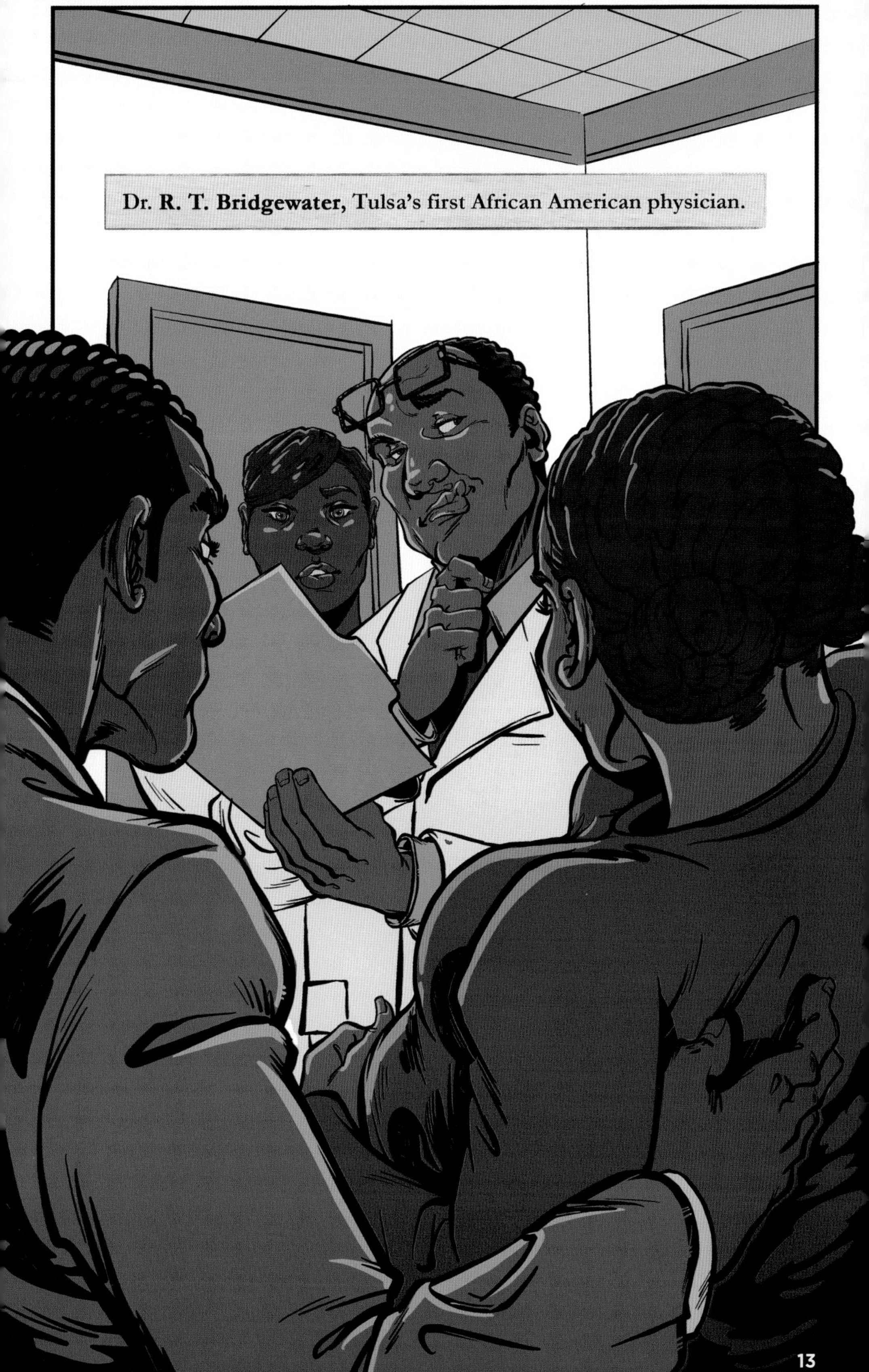
Dr. R. T. Bridgewater, Tulsa's first African American physician.

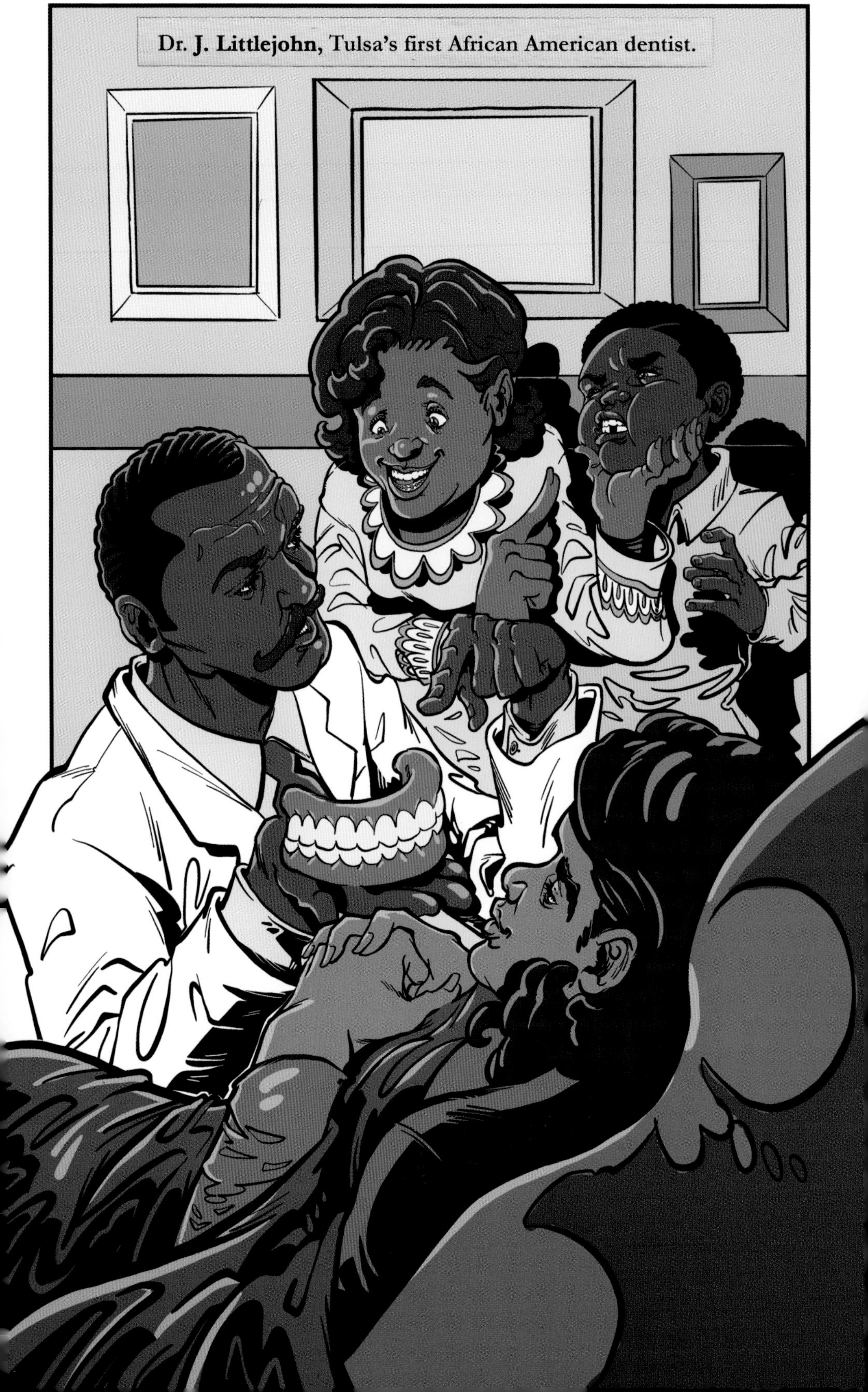
Dr. J. Littlejohn, Tulsa's first African American dentist.

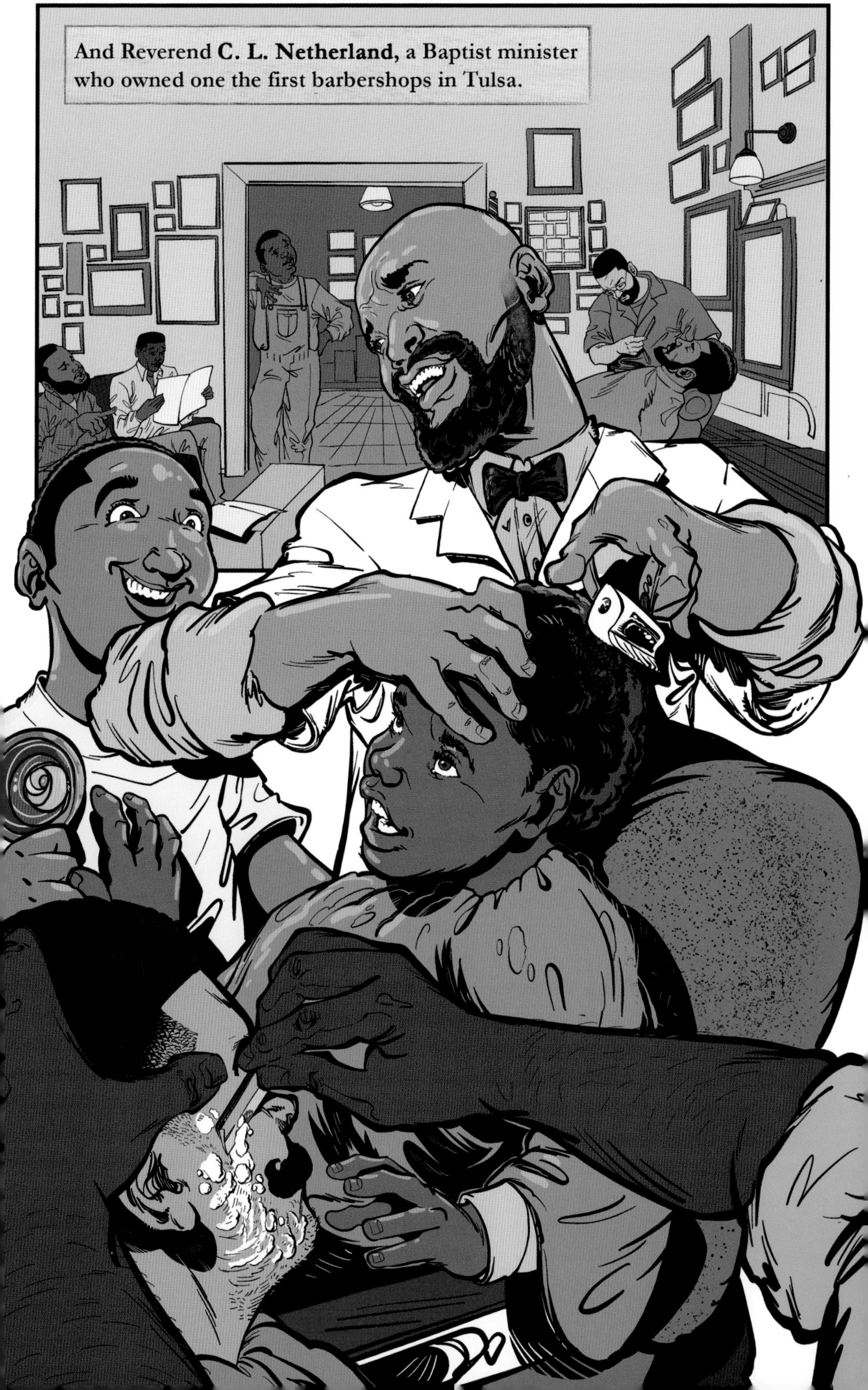
And Reverend **C. L. Netherland,** a Baptist minister who owned one the first barbershops in Tulsa.

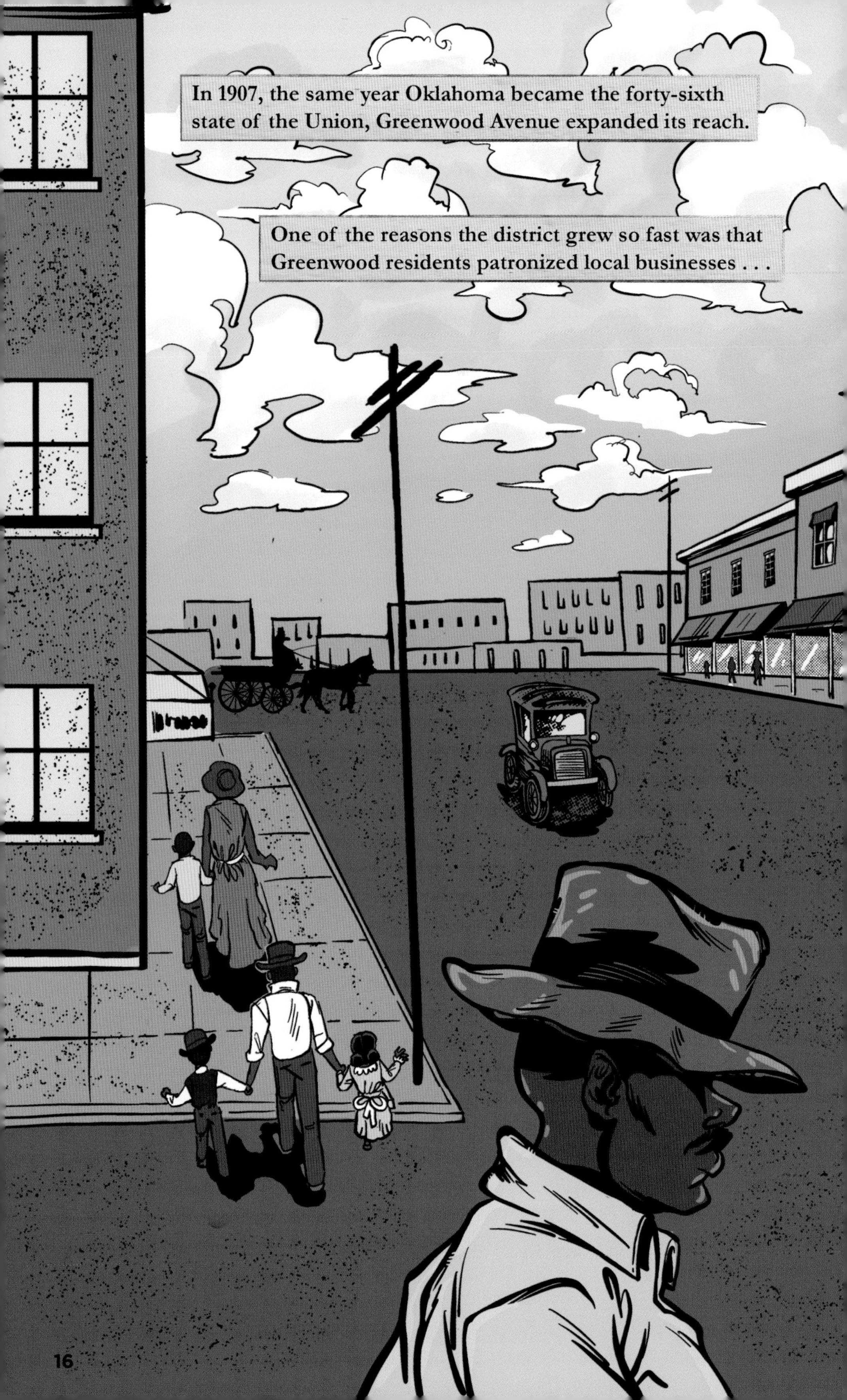
In 1907, the same year Oklahoma became the forty-sixth state of the Union, Greenwood Avenue expanded its reach.
One of the reasons the district grew so fast was that Greenwood residents patronized local businesses . . .

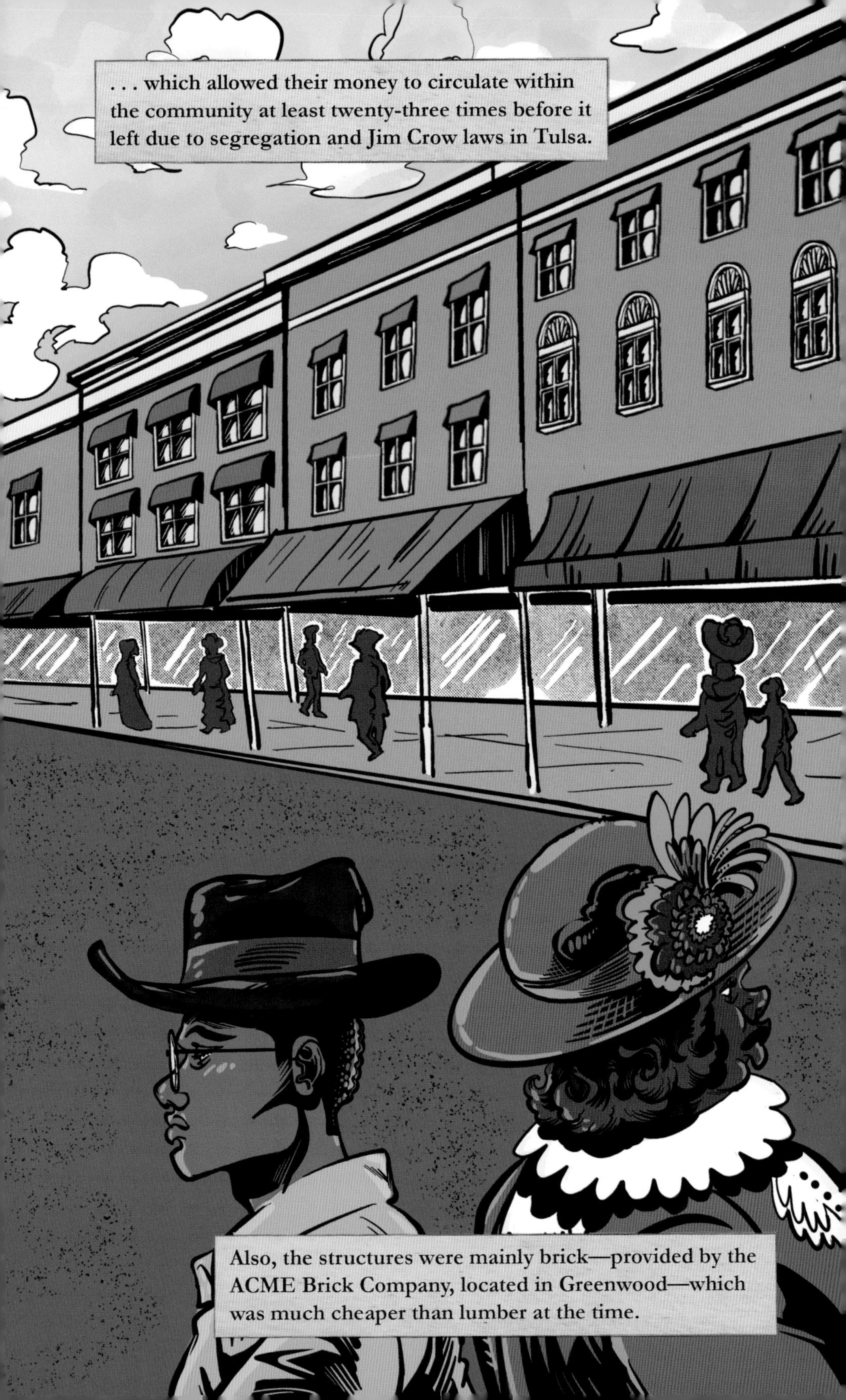
. . . which allowed their money to circulate within the community at least twenty-three times before it left due to segregation and Jim Crow laws in Tulsa.
Also, the structures were mainly brick—provided by the ACME Brick Company, located in Greenwood—which was much cheaper than lumber at the time.

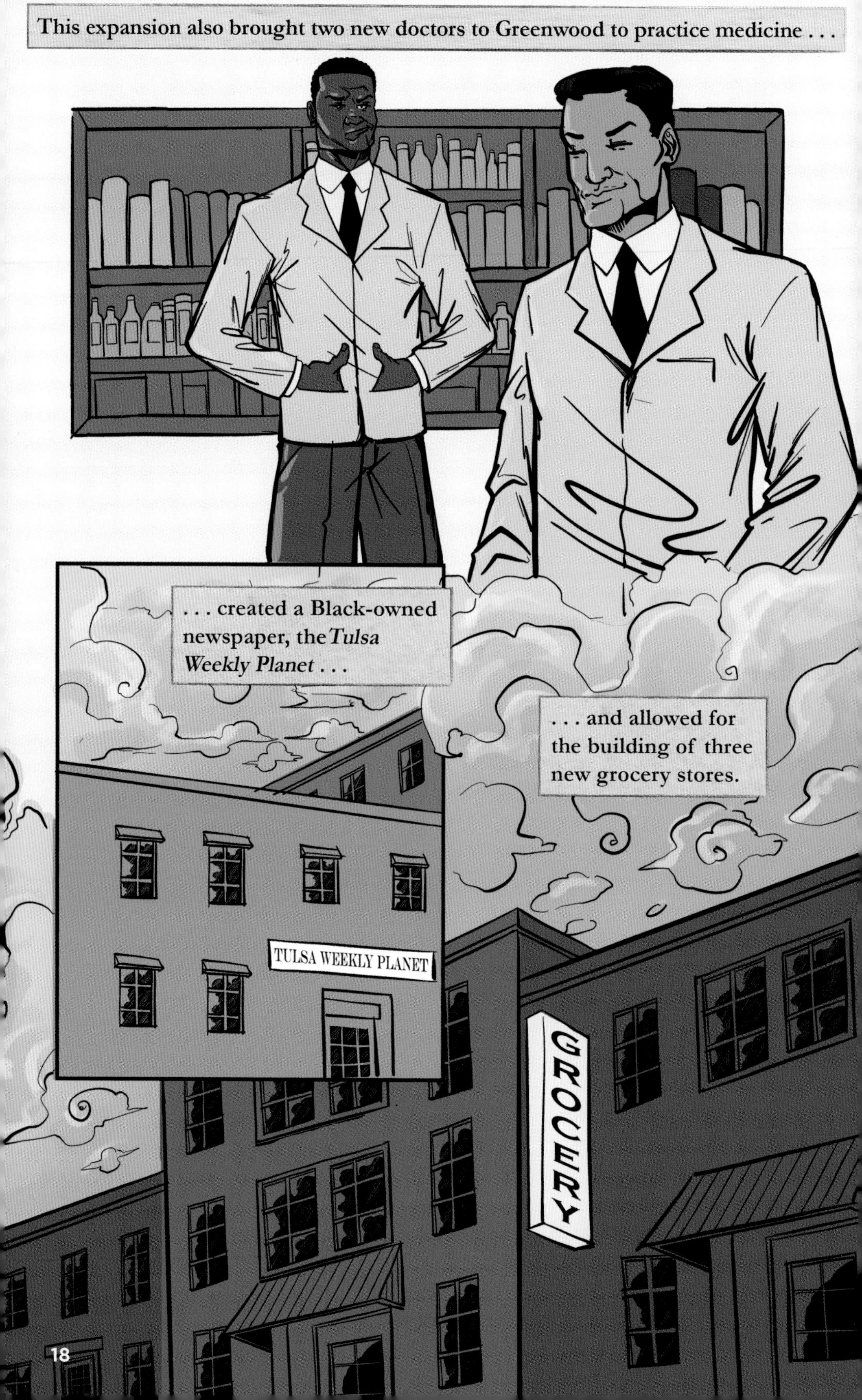
This expansion also brought two new doctors to Greenwood to practice medicine . . .
. . . created a Black-owned newspaper, the *Tulsa Weekly Planet* . . .
TULSA WEEKLY PLANET
. . . and allowed for the building of three new grocery stores.
GROCERY

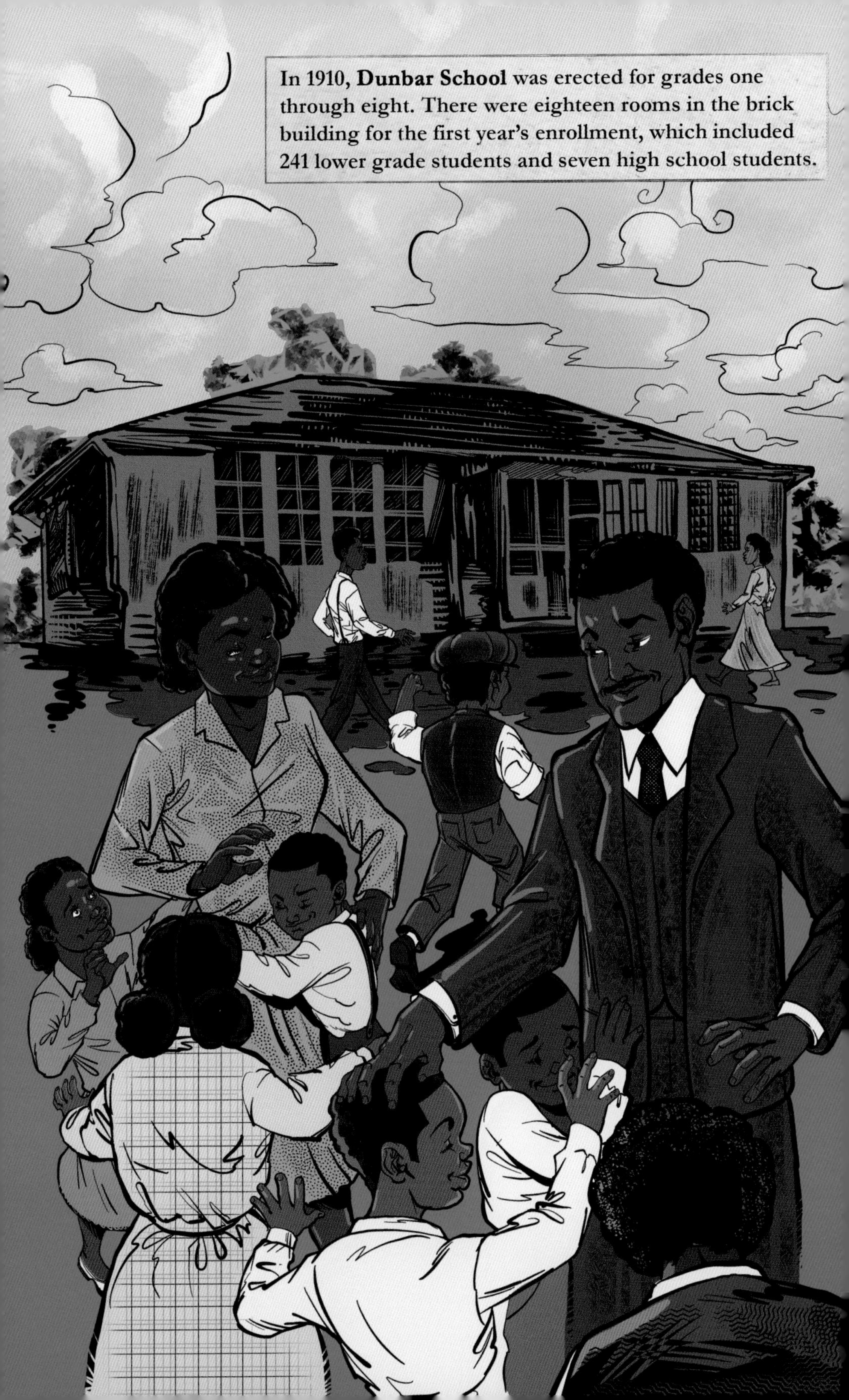
In 1910, **Dunbar School** was erected for grades one through eight. There were eighteen rooms in the brick building for the first year's enrollment, which included 241 lower grade students and seven high school students.

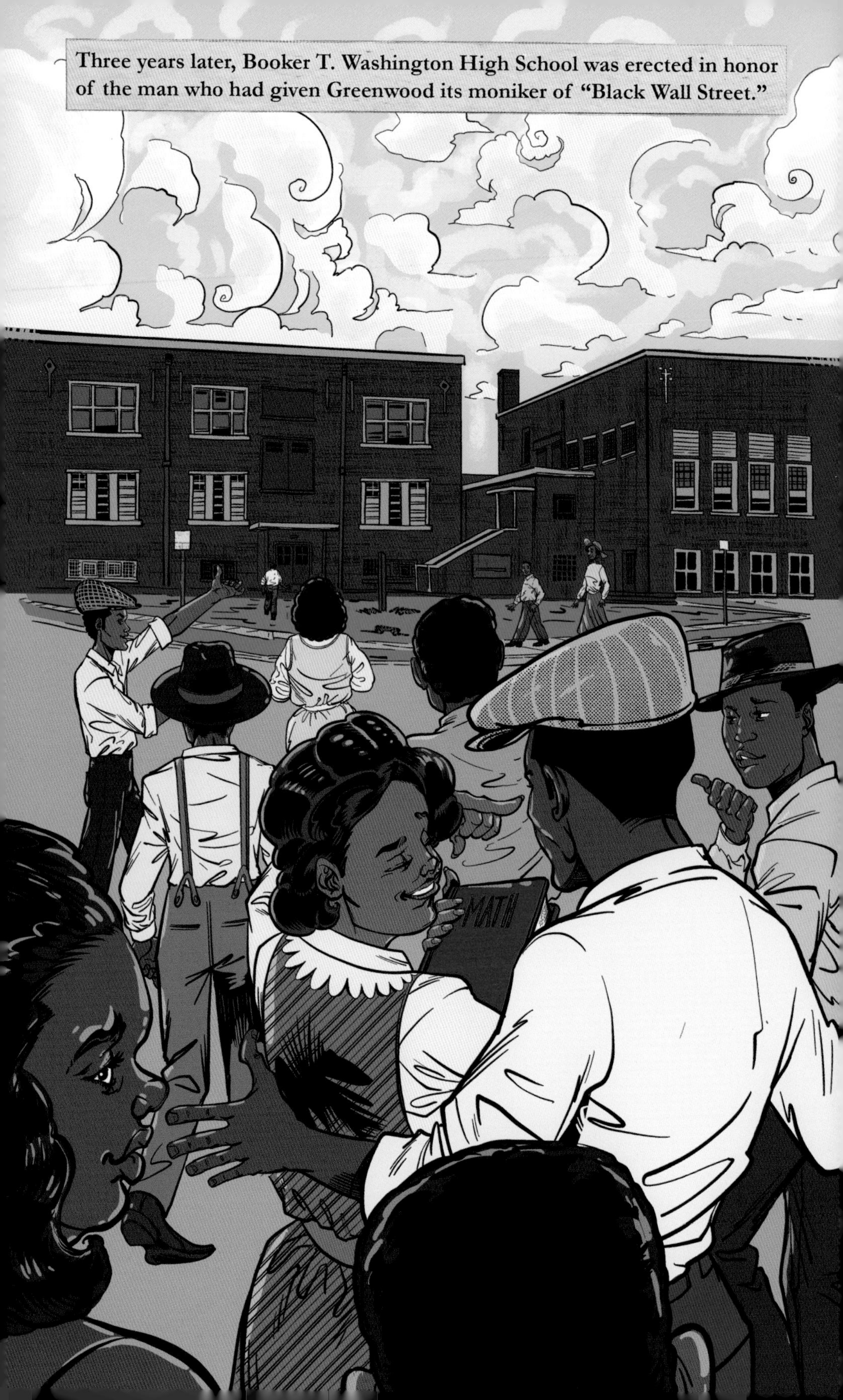
Three years later, Booker T. Washington High School was erected in honor of the man who had given Greenwood its moniker of "Black Wall Street."
MATH

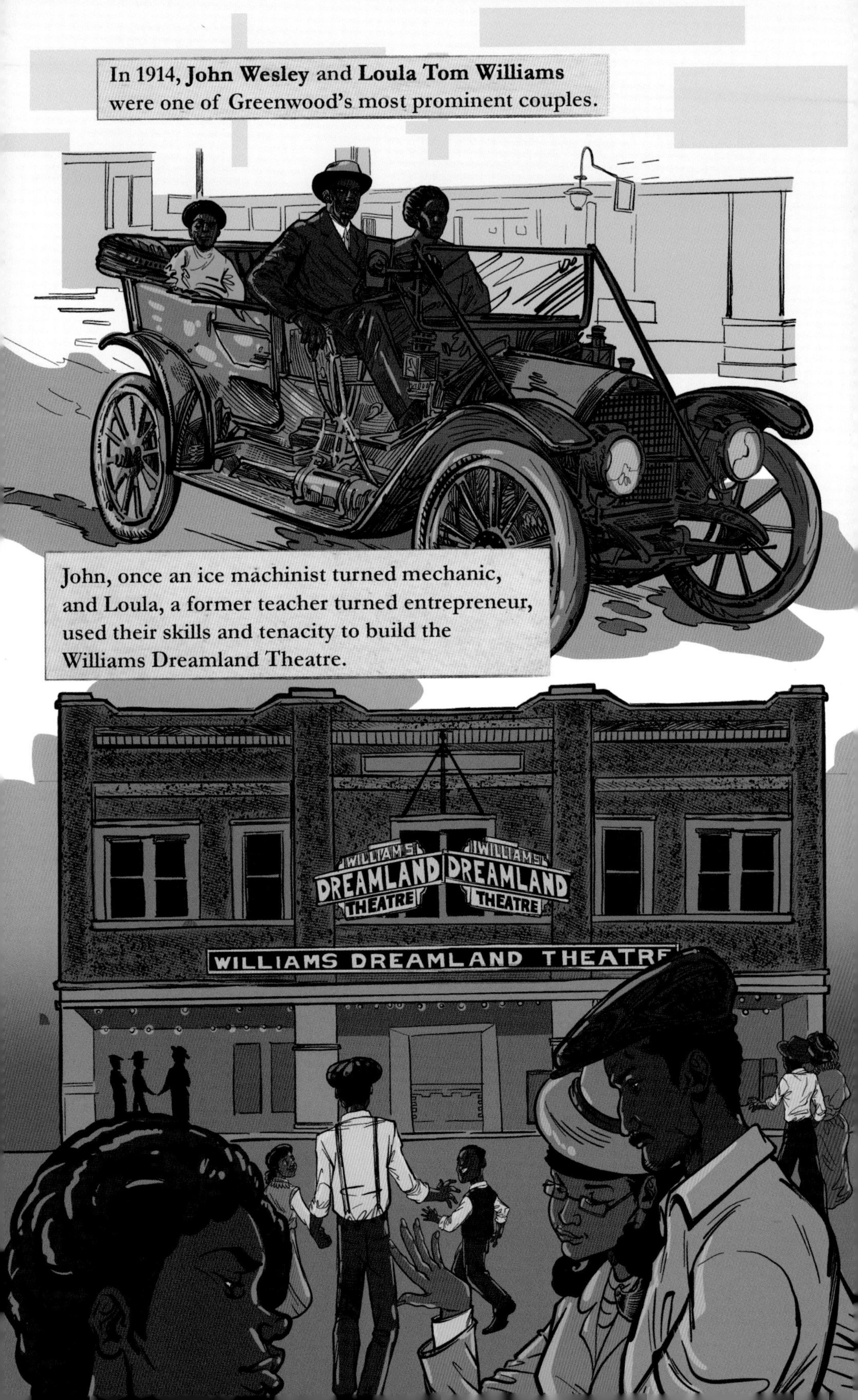
In 1914, **John Wesley** and **Loula Tom Williams** were one of Greenwood's most prominent couples.
John, once an ice machinist turned mechanic, and Loula, a former teacher turned entrepreneur, used their skills and tenacity to build the Williams Dreamland Theatre.
WILLIAMS DREAMLAND THEATRE
WILLIAMS DREAMLAND THEATRE
WILLIAMS DREAMLAND THEATR

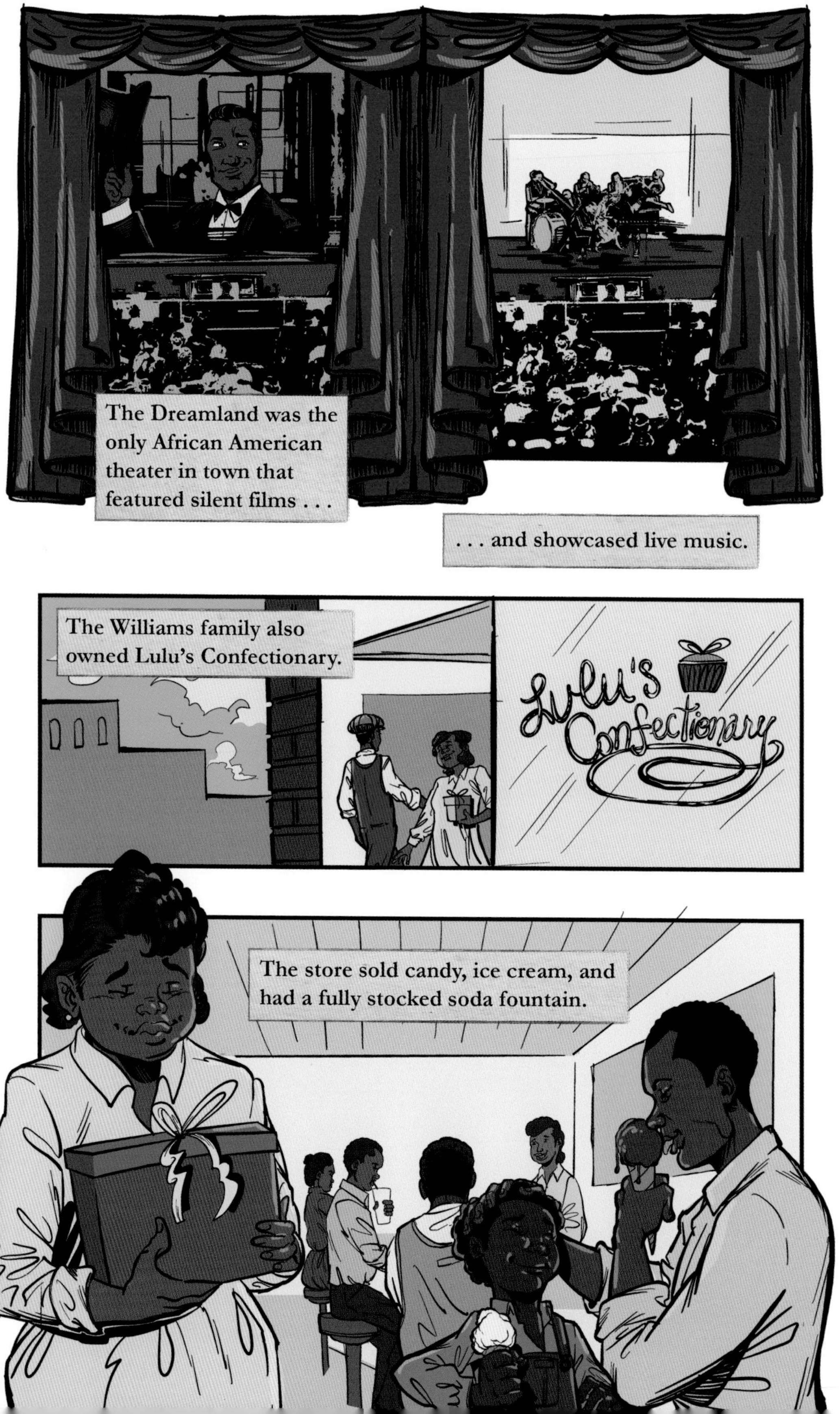
The Dreamland was the only African American theater in town that featured silent films . . .
. . . and showcased live music.
The Williams family also owned Lulu's Confectionary.
Lulu's Confectionary
The store sold candy, ice cream, and had a fully stocked soda fountain.

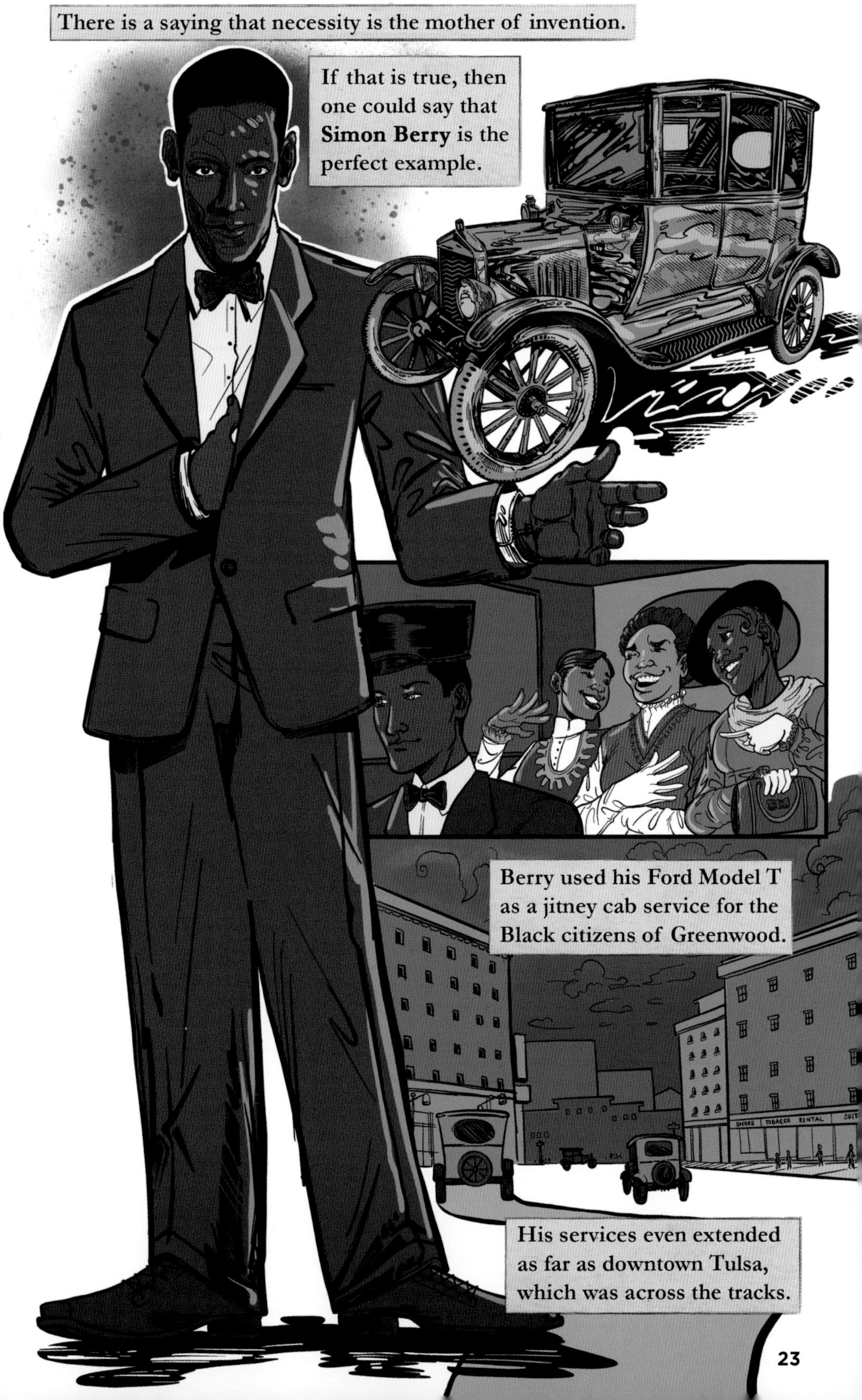
There is a saying that necessity is the mother of invention.
If that is true, then one could say that **Simon Berry** is the perfect example.
Berry used his Ford Model T as a jitney cab service for the Black citizens of Greenwood.
His services even extended as far as downtown Tulsa, which was across the tracks.

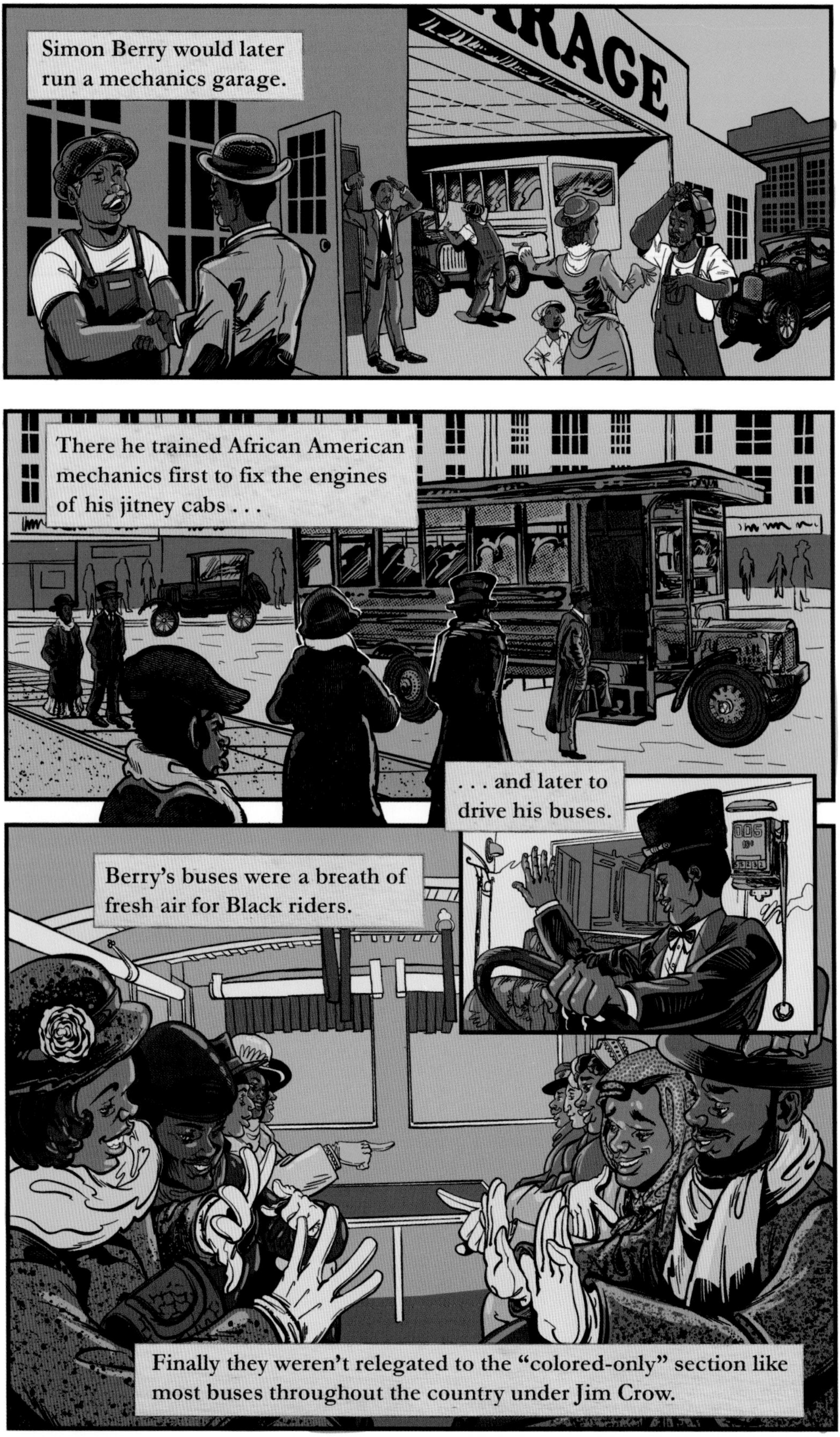
Simon Berry would later run a mechanics garage.
ARAGE
There he trained African American mechanics first to fix the engines of his jitney cabs . . .
. . . and later to drive his buses.
Berry's buses were a breath of fresh air for Black riders.
Finally they weren't relegated to the "colored-only" section like most buses throughout the country under Jim Crow.

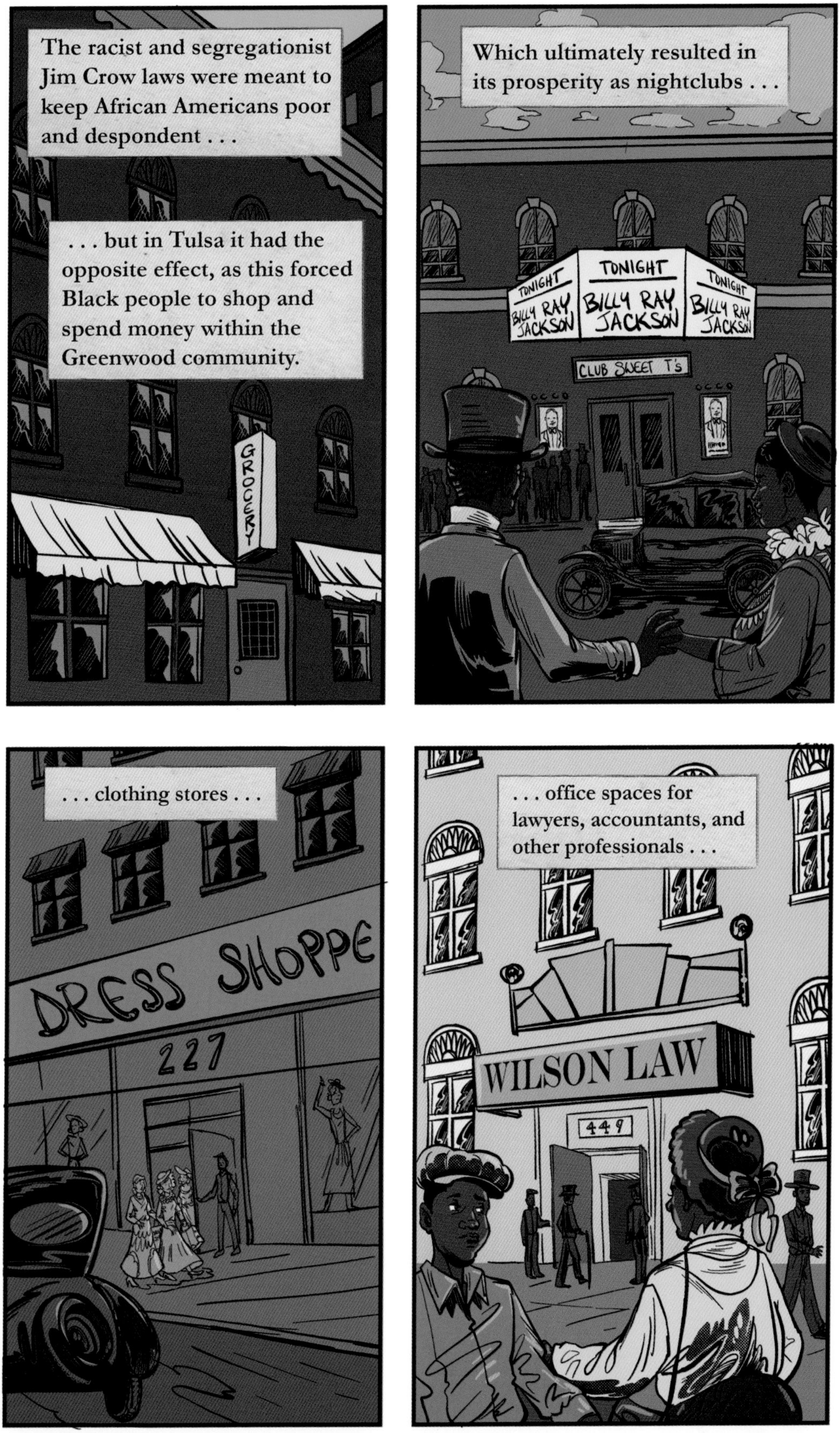
The racist and segregationist Jim Crow laws were meant to keep African Americans poor and despondent . . .
. . . but in Tulsa it had the opposite effect, as this forced Black people to shop and spend money within the Greenwood community.
GROCERY
Which ultimately resulted in its prosperity as nightclubs . . .
TONIGHT BILLY RAY JACKSON
TONIGHT BILLY RAY JACKSON
TONIGHT BILLY RAY JACKSON
CLUB SWEET T's
. . . clothing stores . . .
DRESS SHOPPE
227
. . . office spaces for lawyers, accountants, and other professionals . . .
WILSON LAW
449

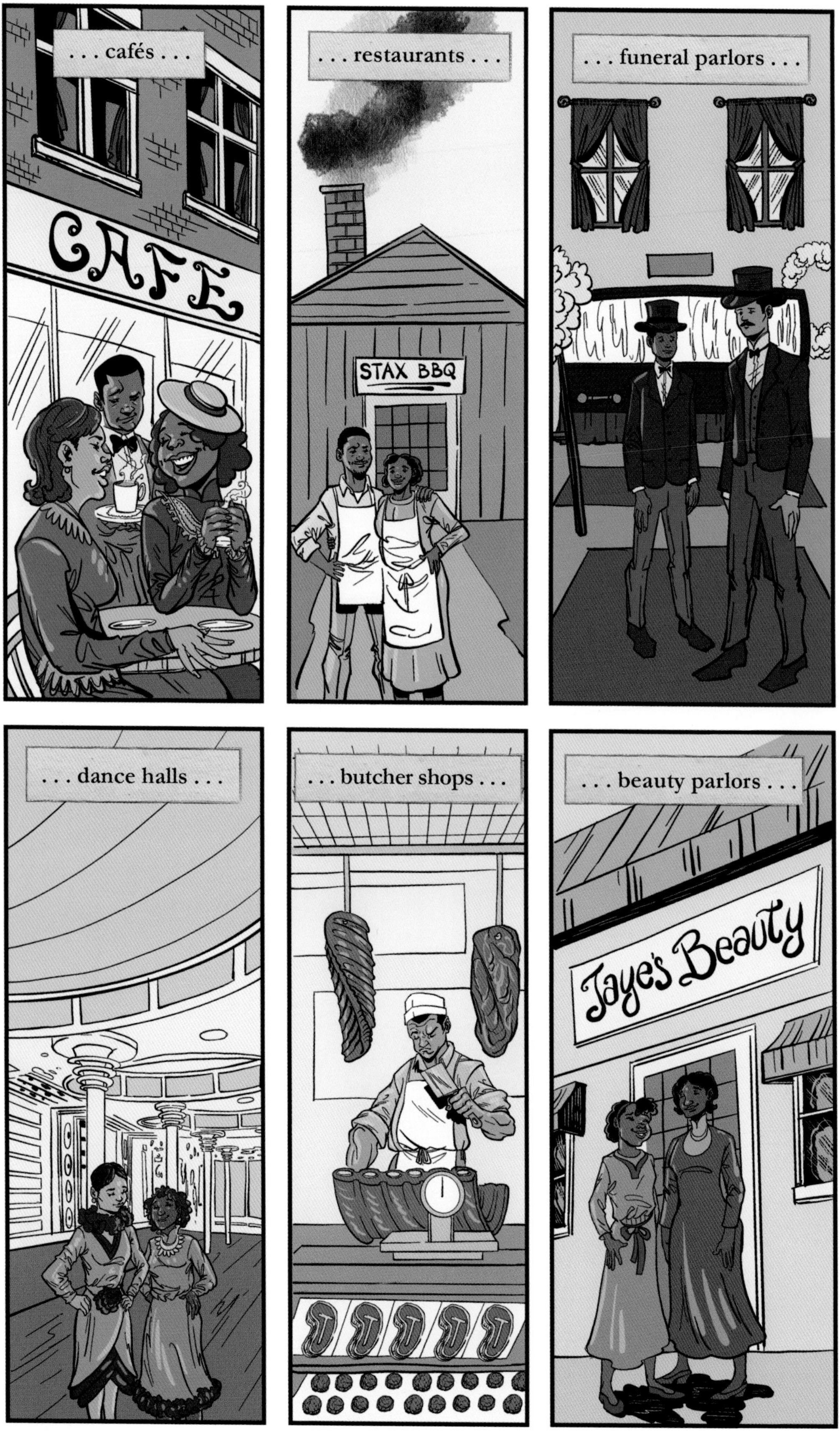
. . . cafés . . .
CAFE
. . . restaurants . . .
STAX BBQ
. . . funeral parlors . . .
. . . dance halls . . .
. . . butcher shops . . .
. . . beauty parlors . . .
Jaye's Beauty

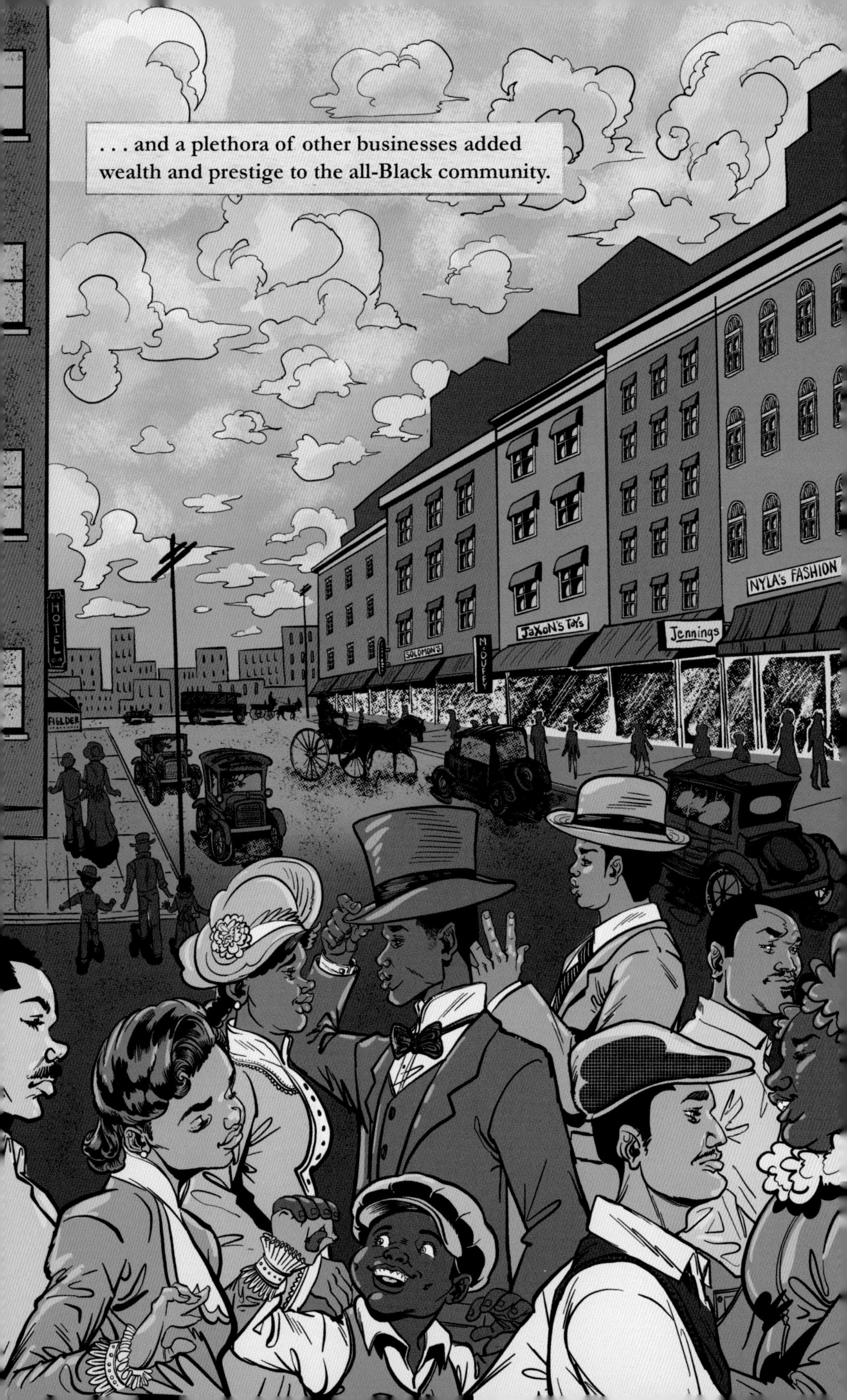
. . . and a plethora of other businesses added wealth and prestige to the all-Black community.
HOTEL
FIELDER
SOLOMON'S
McDUFFY
JAXON'S TOYS
Jennings
NYLA's FASHION

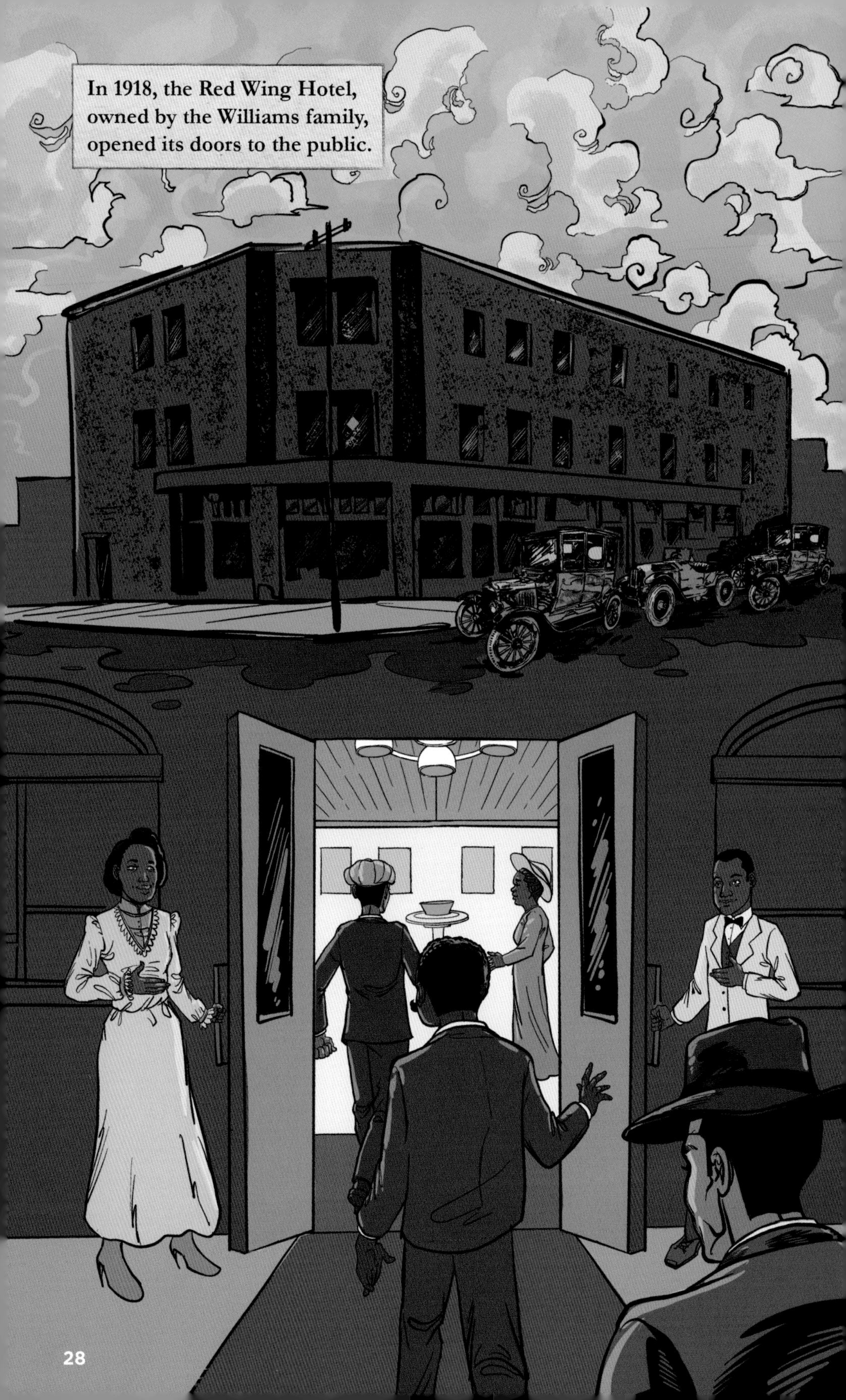
In 1918, the Red Wing Hotel, owned by the Williams family, opened its doors to the public.

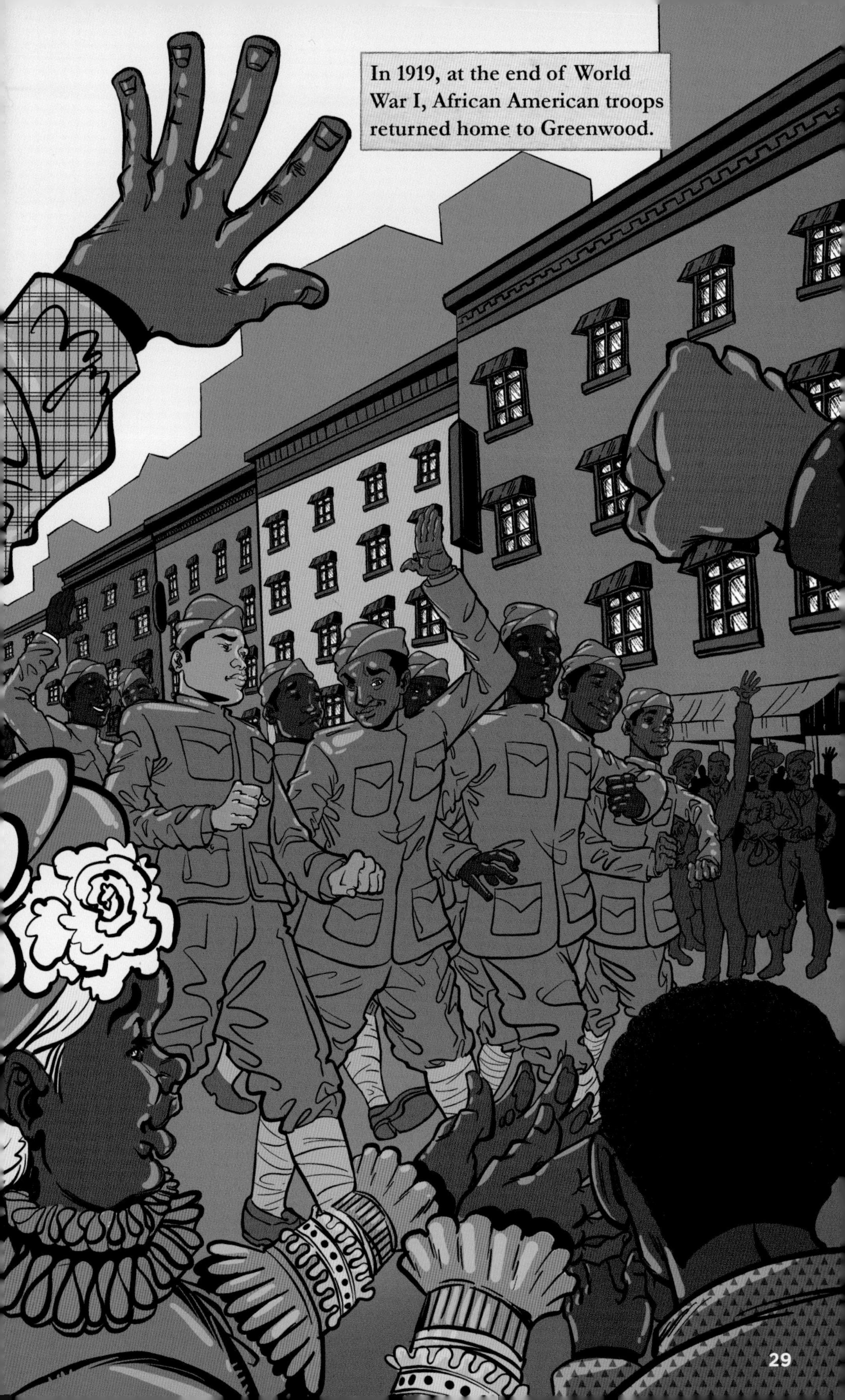
In 1919, at the end of World War I, African American troops returned home to Greenwood.

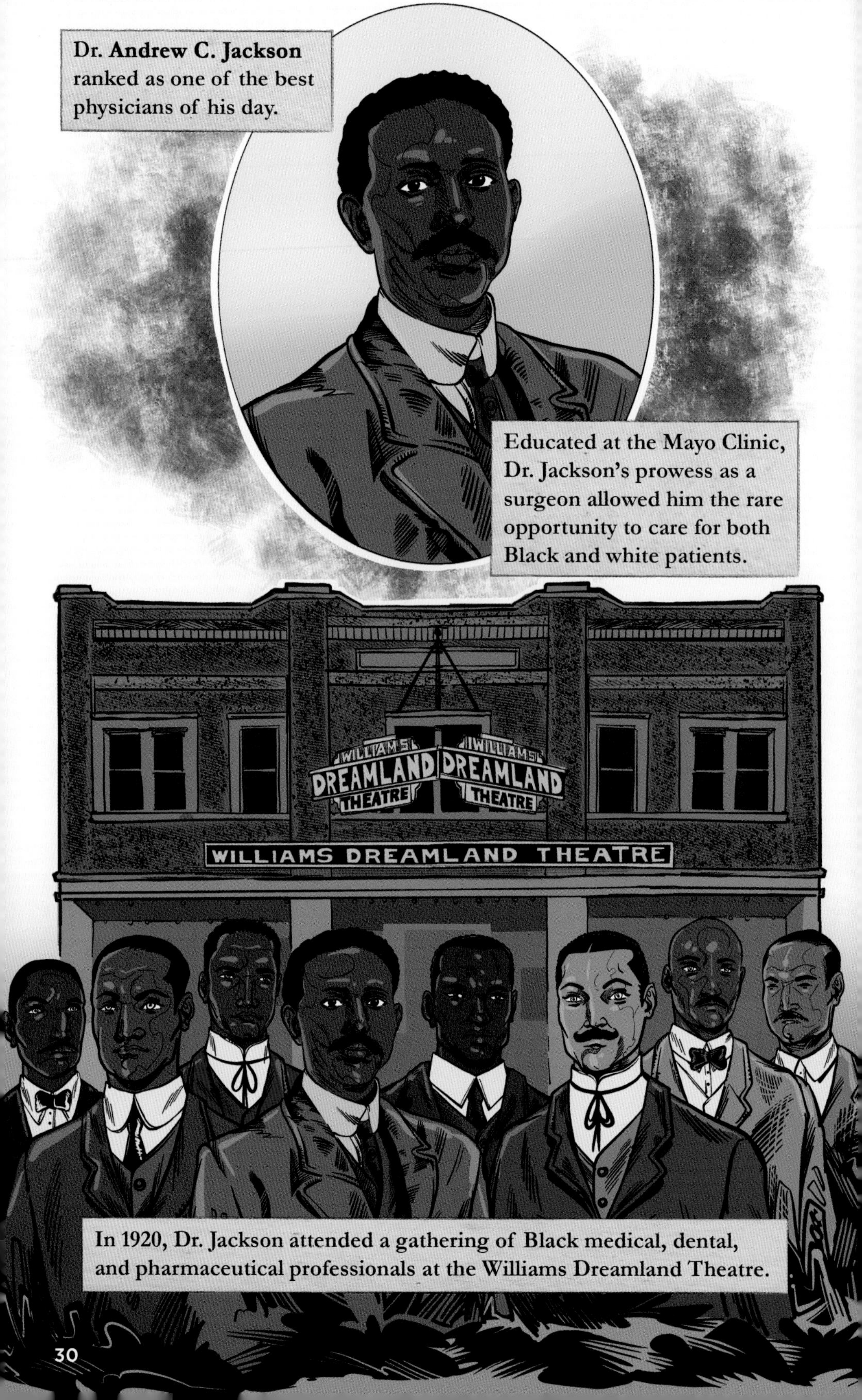
Dr. Andrew C. Jackson ranked as one of the best physicians of his day.
Educated at the Mayo Clinic, Dr. Jackson's prowess as a surgeon allowed him the rare opportunity to care for both Black and white patients.
WILLIAMS' DREAMLAND THEATRE
WILLIAMS' DREAMLAND THEATRE
WILLIAMS DREAMLAND THEATRE
In 1920, Dr. Jackson attended a gathering of Black medical, dental, and pharmaceutical professionals at the Williams Dreamland Theatre.

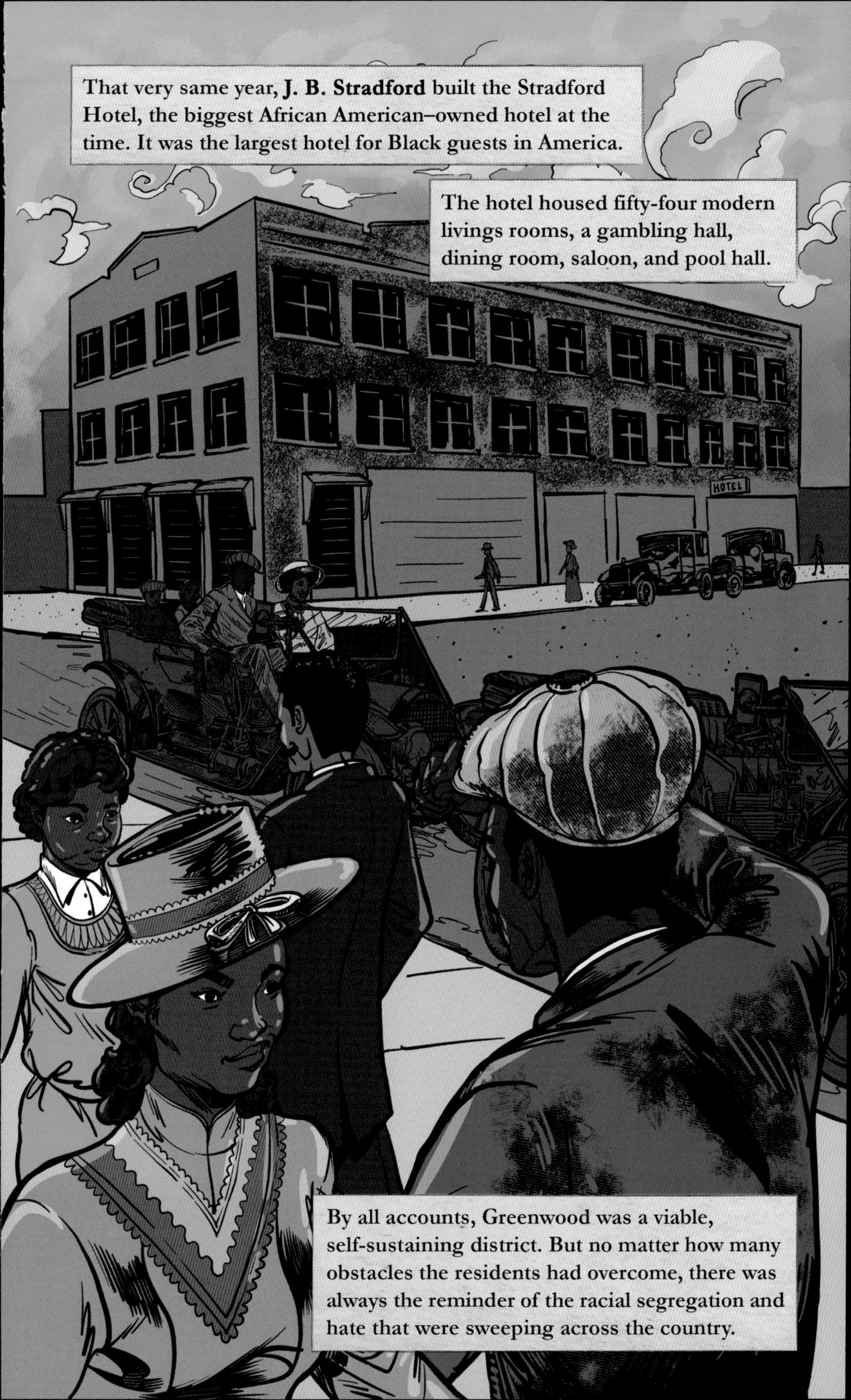
That very same year, **J. B. Stradford** built the Stradford Hotel, the biggest African American–owned hotel at the time. It was the largest hotel for Black guests in America.
The hotel housed fifty-four modern livings rooms, a gambling hall, dining room, saloon, and pool hall.
HOTEL
By all accounts, Greenwood was a viable, self-sustaining district. But no matter how many obstacles the residents had overcome, there was always the reminder of the racial segregation and hate that were sweeping across the country.

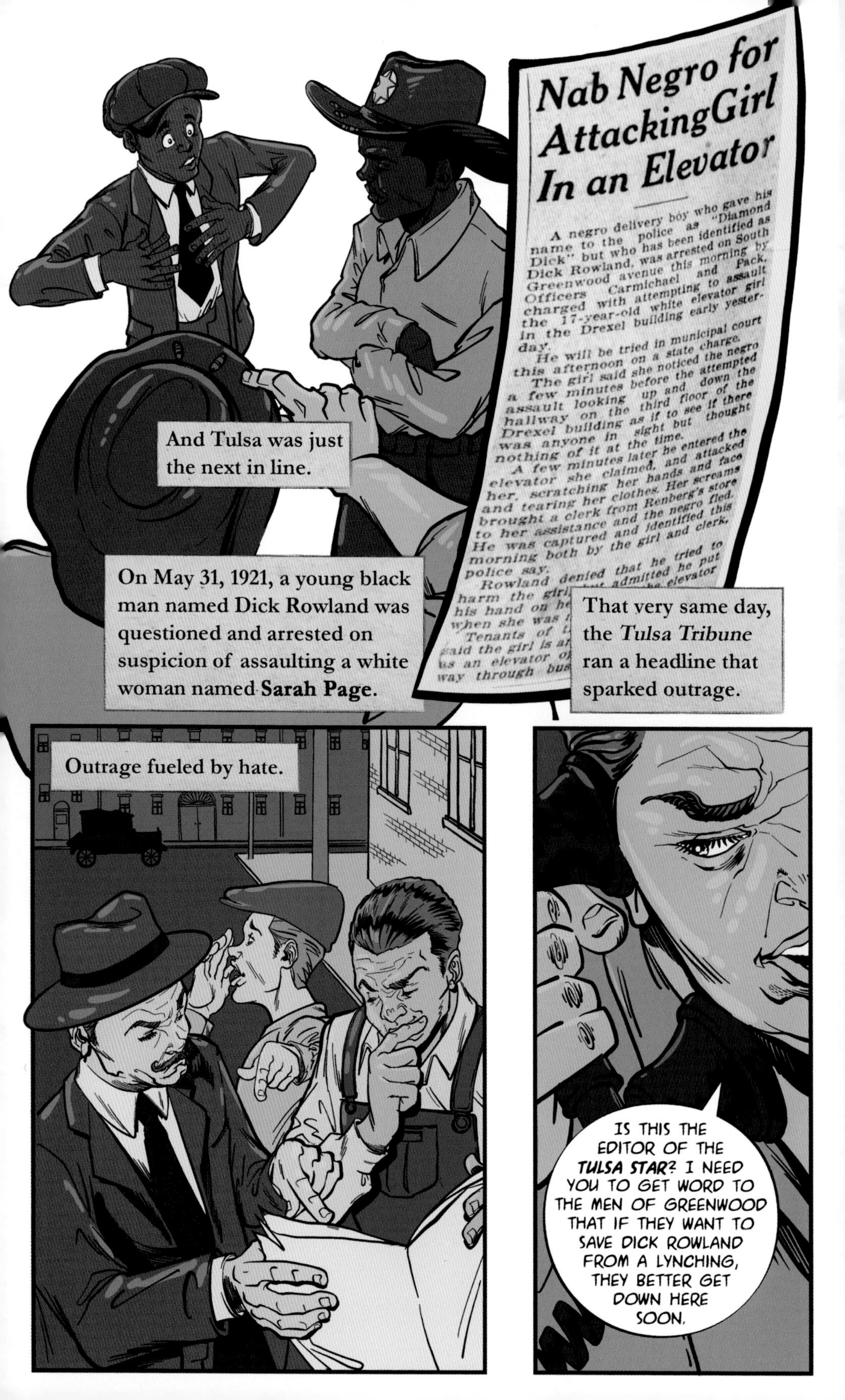
And Tulsa was just the next in line.
On May 31, 1921, a young black man named Dick Rowland was questioned and arrested on suspicion of assaulting a white woman named **Sarah Page**.
That very same day, the *Tulsa Tribune* ran a headline that sparked outrage.
Nab Negro for AttackingGirl In an Elevator
A negro delivery boy who gave his name to the police as "Diamond Dick" but who has been identified as Dick Rowland, was arrested on South Greenwood avenue this morning by Officers Carmichael and Pack, charged with attempting to assault the 17-year-old white elevator girl in the Drexel building early yesterday.
He will be tried in municipal court this afternoon on a state charge.
The girl said she noticed the negro a few minutes before the attempted assault looking up and down the hallway on the third floor of the Drexel building as if to see if there was anyone in sight but thought nothing of it at the time.
A few minutes later he entered the elevator she claimed, and attacked her, scratching her hands and face and tearing her clothes. Her screams brought a clerk from Renberg's store to her assistance and the negro fled. He was captured and identified this morning both by the girl and clerk, police say.
Rowland denied that he tried to
Outrage fueled by hate.
IS THIS THE EDITOR OF THE ***TULSA STAR***? I NEED YOU TO GET WORD TO THE MEN OF GREENWOOD THAT IF THEY WANT TO SAVE DICK ROWLAND FROM A LYNCHING, THEY BETTER GET DOWN HERE SOON.

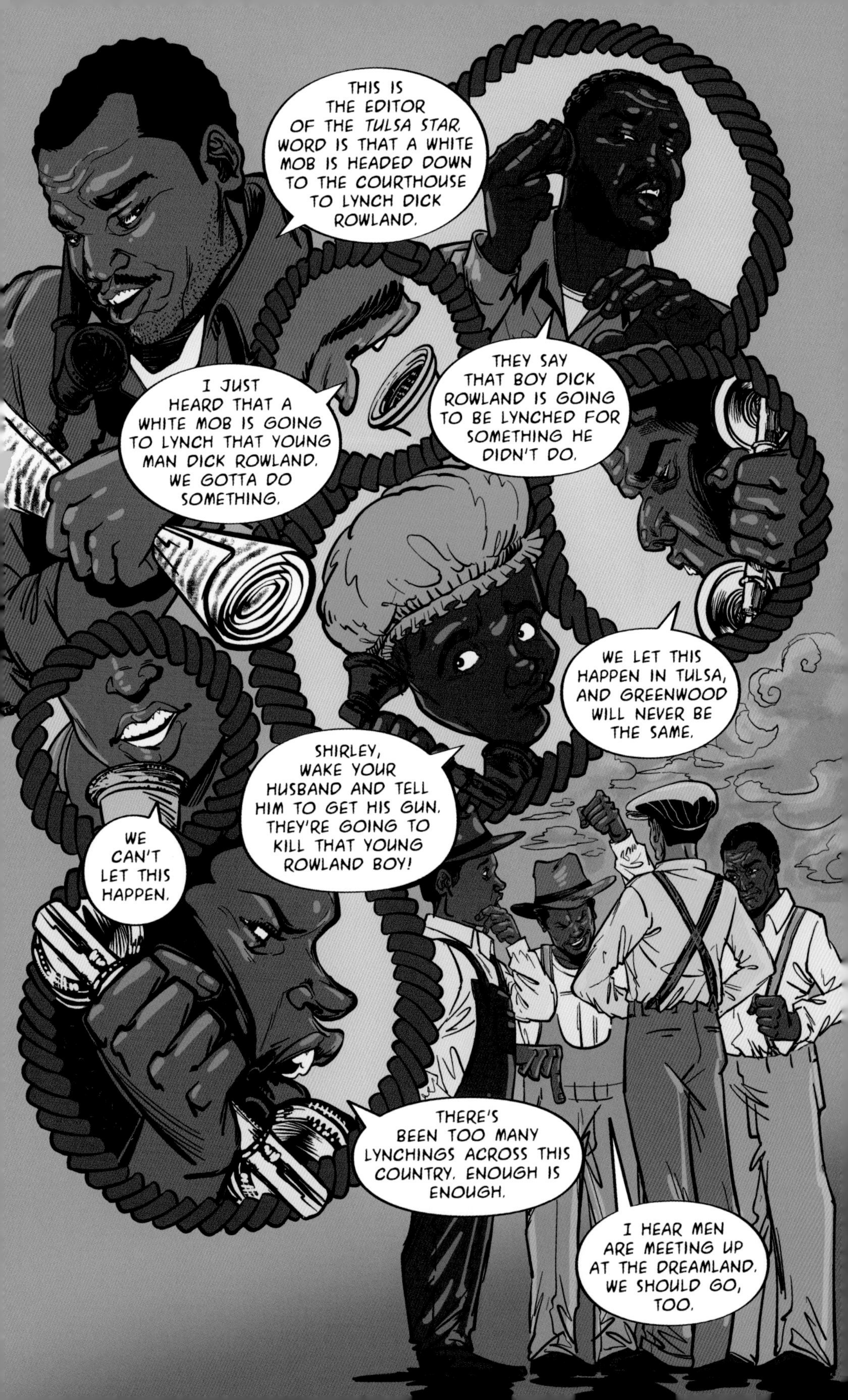
THIS IS THE EDITOR OF THE TULSA STAR. WORD IS THAT A WHITE MOB IS HEADED DOWN TO THE COURTHOUSE TO LYNCH DICK ROWLAND.
I JUST HEARD THAT A WHITE MOB IS GOING TO LYNCH THAT YOUNG MAN DICK ROWLAND. WE GOTTA DO SOMETHING.
THEY SAY THAT BOY DICK ROWLAND IS GOING TO BE LYNCHED FOR SOMETHING HE DIDN'T DO.
WE LET THIS HAPPEN IN TULSA, AND GREENWOOD WILL NEVER BE THE SAME.
SHIRLEY, WAKE YOUR HUSBAND AND TELL HIM TO GET HIS GUN. THEY'RE GOING TO KILL THAT YOUNG ROWLAND BOY!
WE CAN'T LET THIS HAPPEN.
THERE'S BEEN TOO MANY LYNCHINGS ACROSS THIS COUNTRY. ENOUGH IS ENOUGH.
I HEAR MEN ARE MEETING UP AT THE DREAMLAND. WE SHOULD GO, TOO.

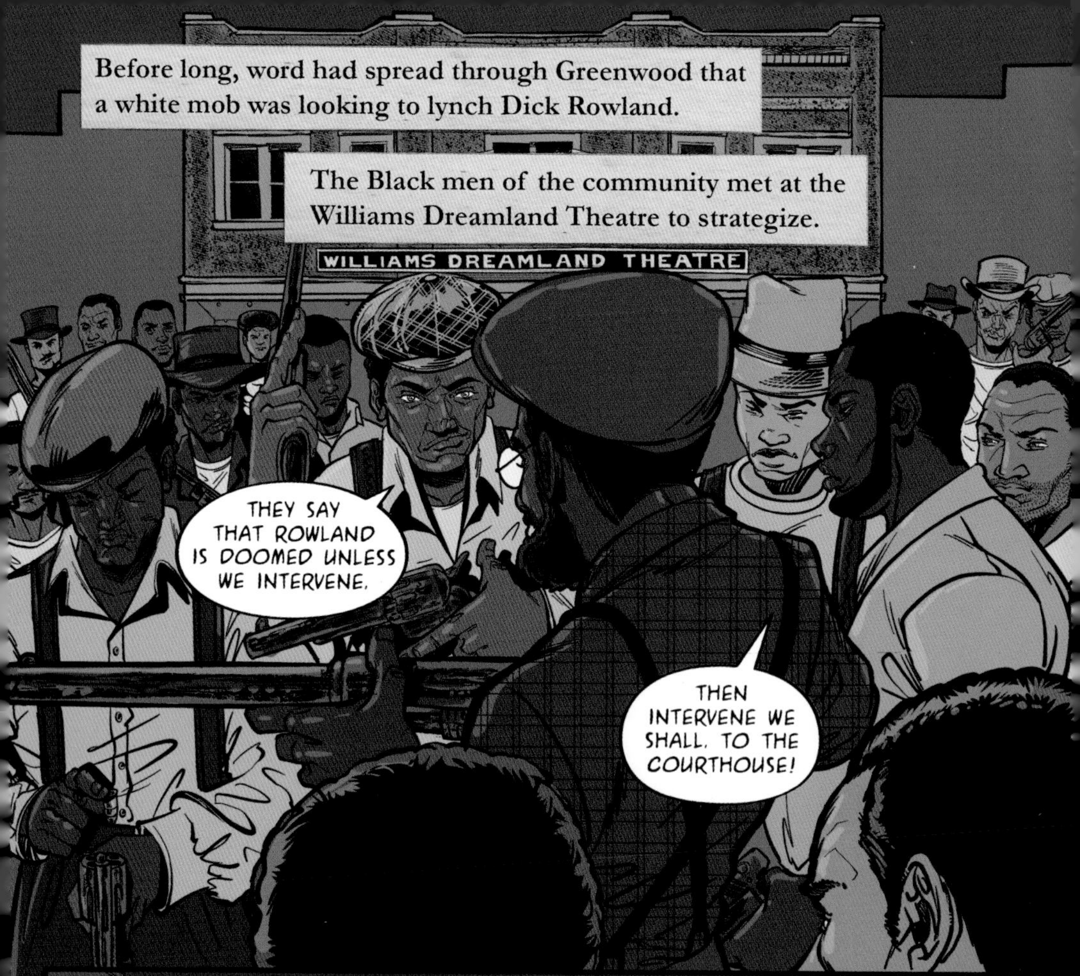
Before long, word had spread through Greenwood that a white mob was looking to lynch Dick Rowland.
The Black men of the community met at the Williams Dreamland Theatre to strategize.
WILLIAMS DREAMLAND THEATRE
THEY SAY THAT ROWLAND IS DOOMED UNLESS WE INTERVENE.
THEN INTERVENE WE SHALL. TO THE COURTHOUSE!

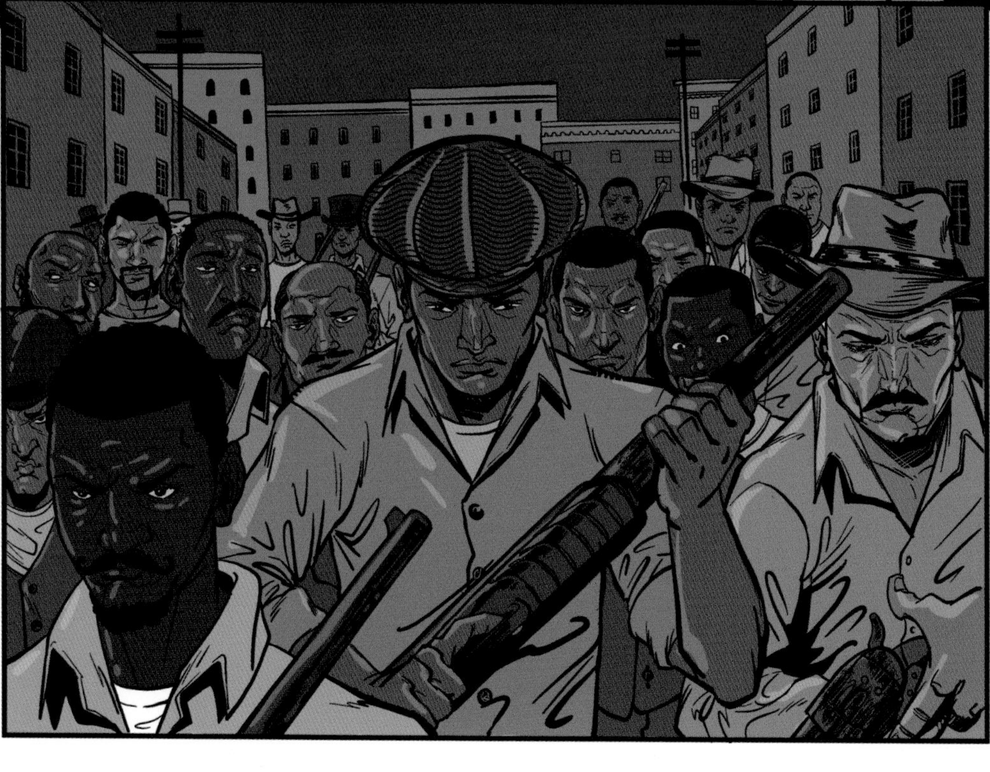

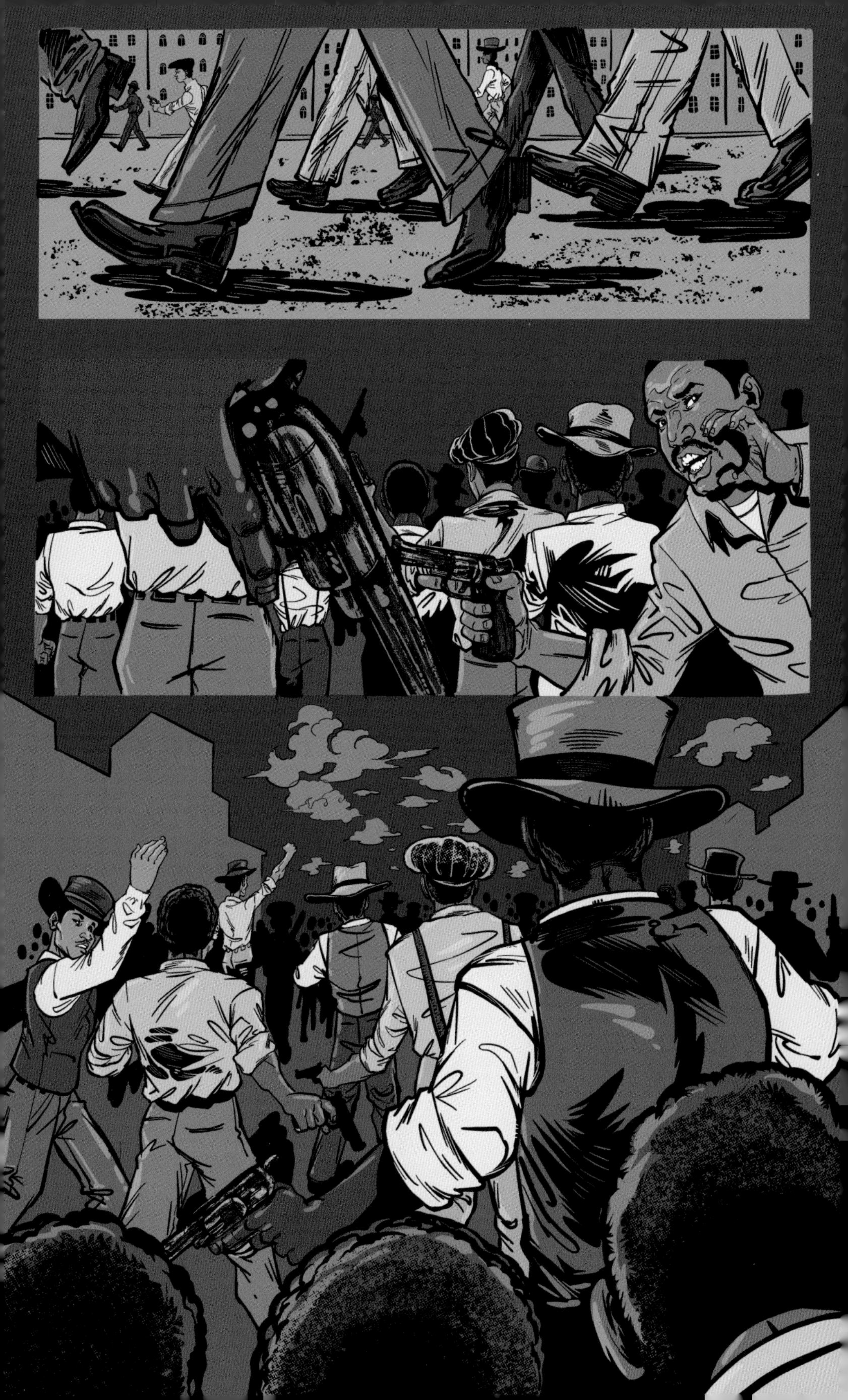

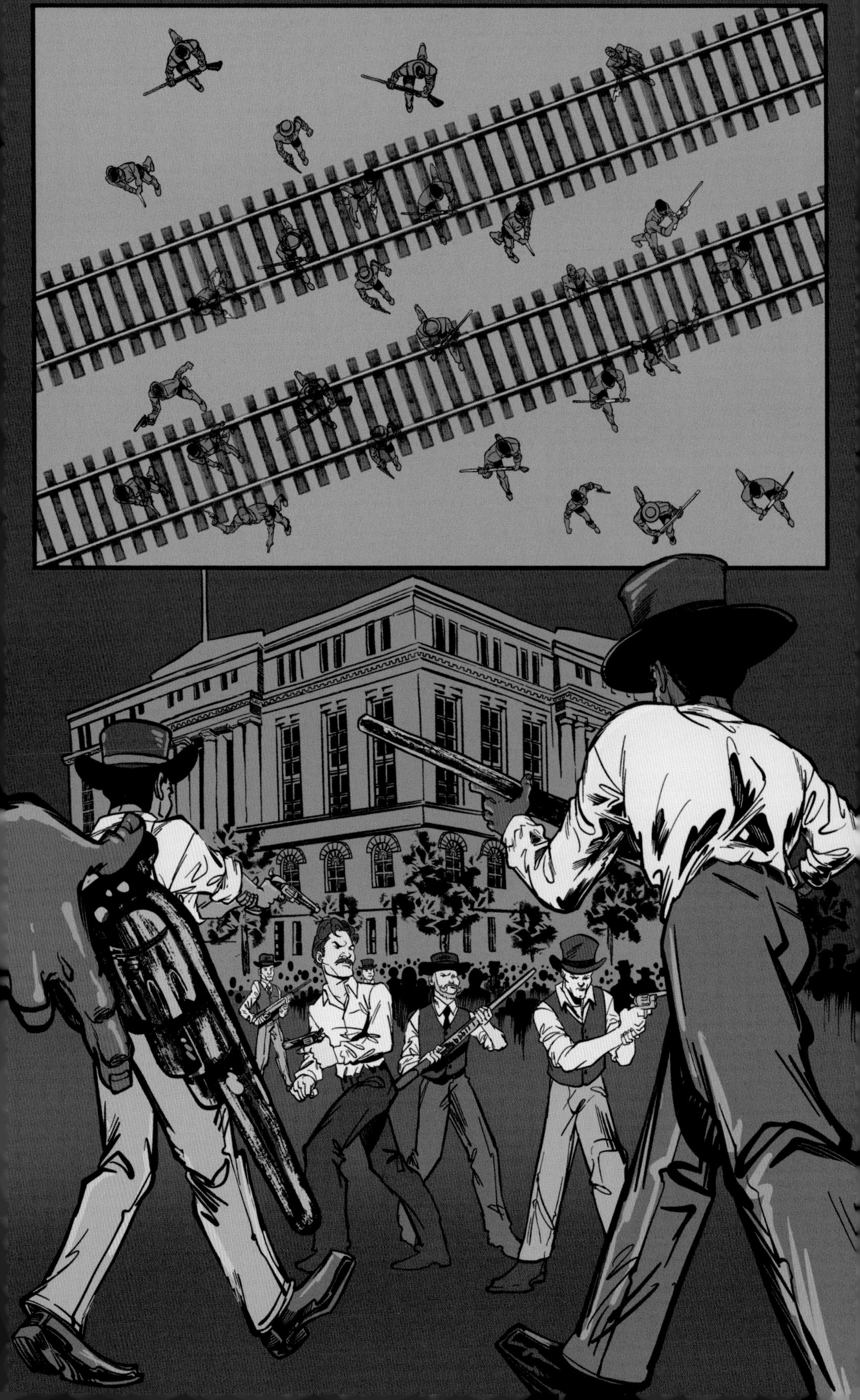

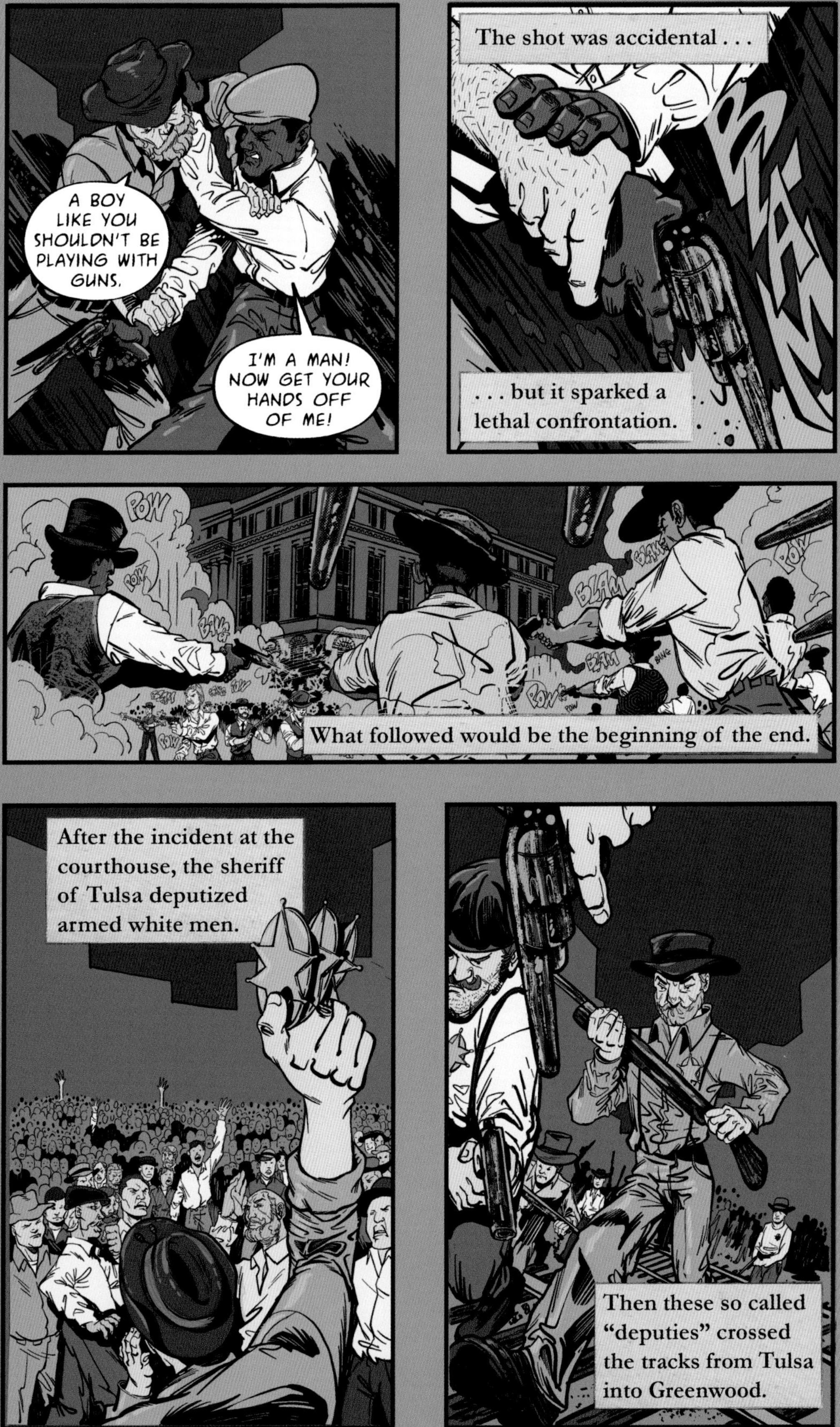
A BOY LIKE YOU SHOULDN'T BE PLAYING WITH GUNS.
I'M A MAN! NOW GET YOUR HANDS OFF OF ME!
The shot was accidental . . .
. . . but it sparked a lethal confrontation.
POW
BLAM
POW
What followed would be the beginning of the end.
After the incident at the courthouse, the sheriff of Tulsa deputized armed white men.
Then these so called "deputies" crossed the tracks from Tulsa into Greenwood.

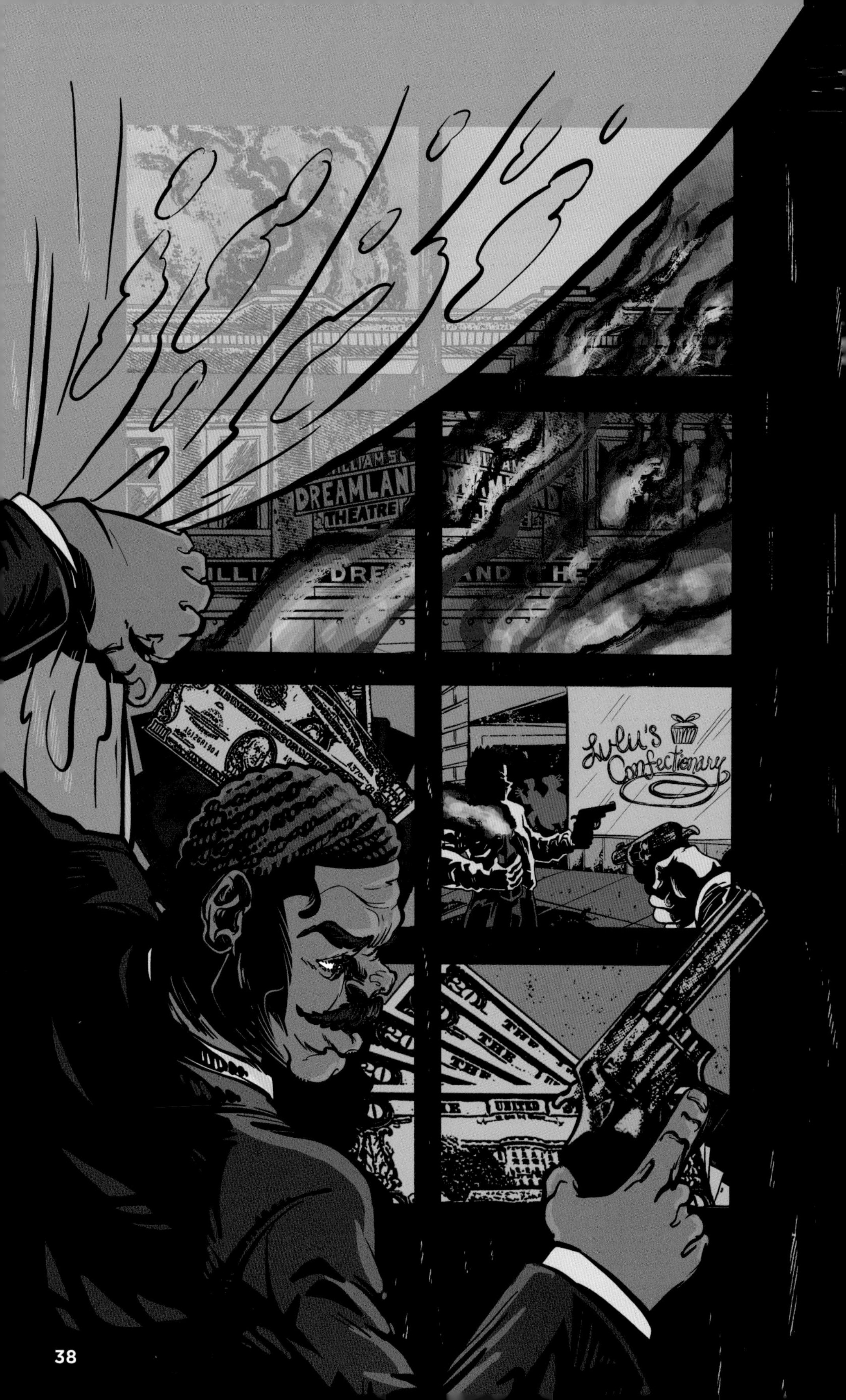
DREAMLAN
THEATRE
Lulu's Confectionary

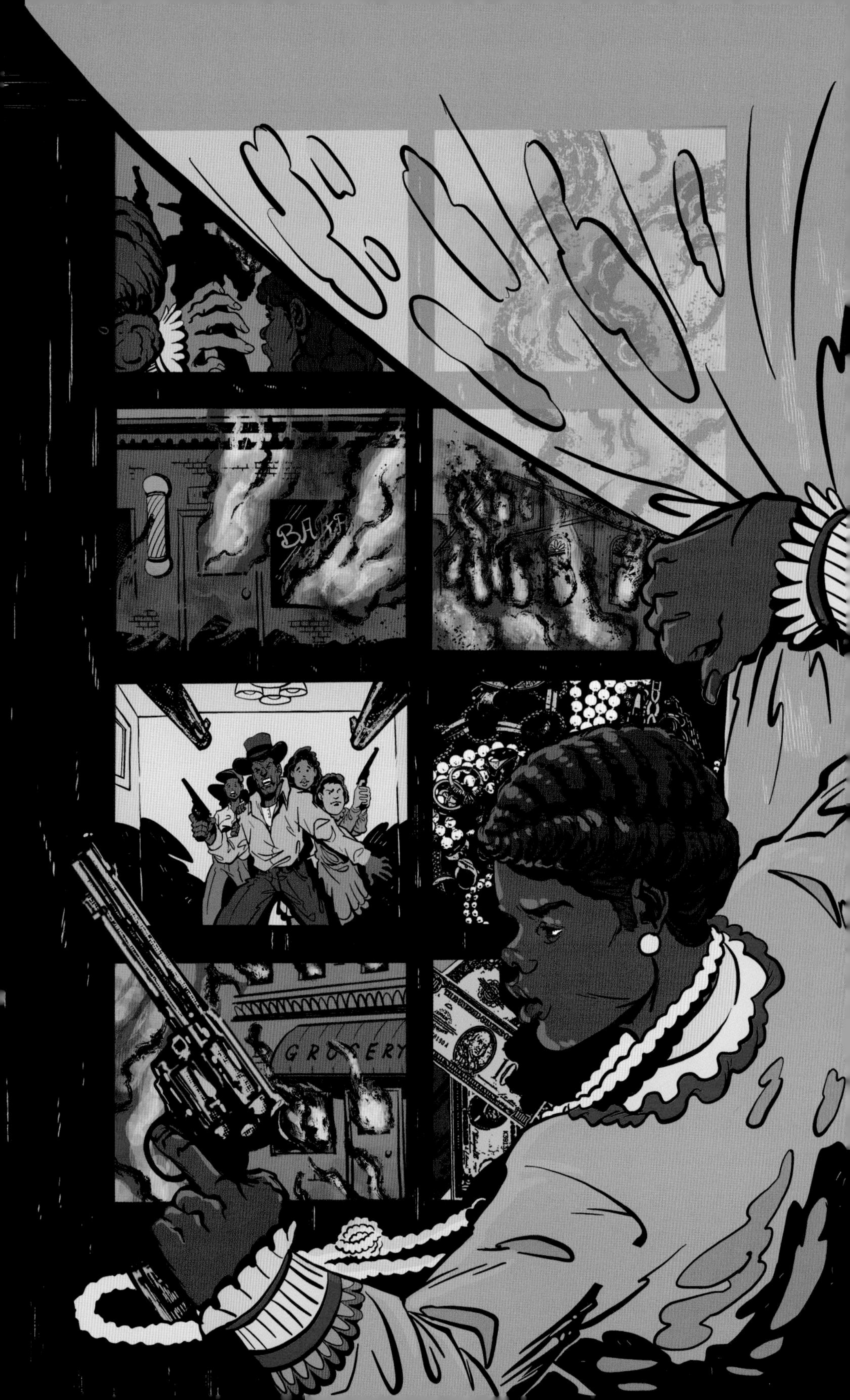

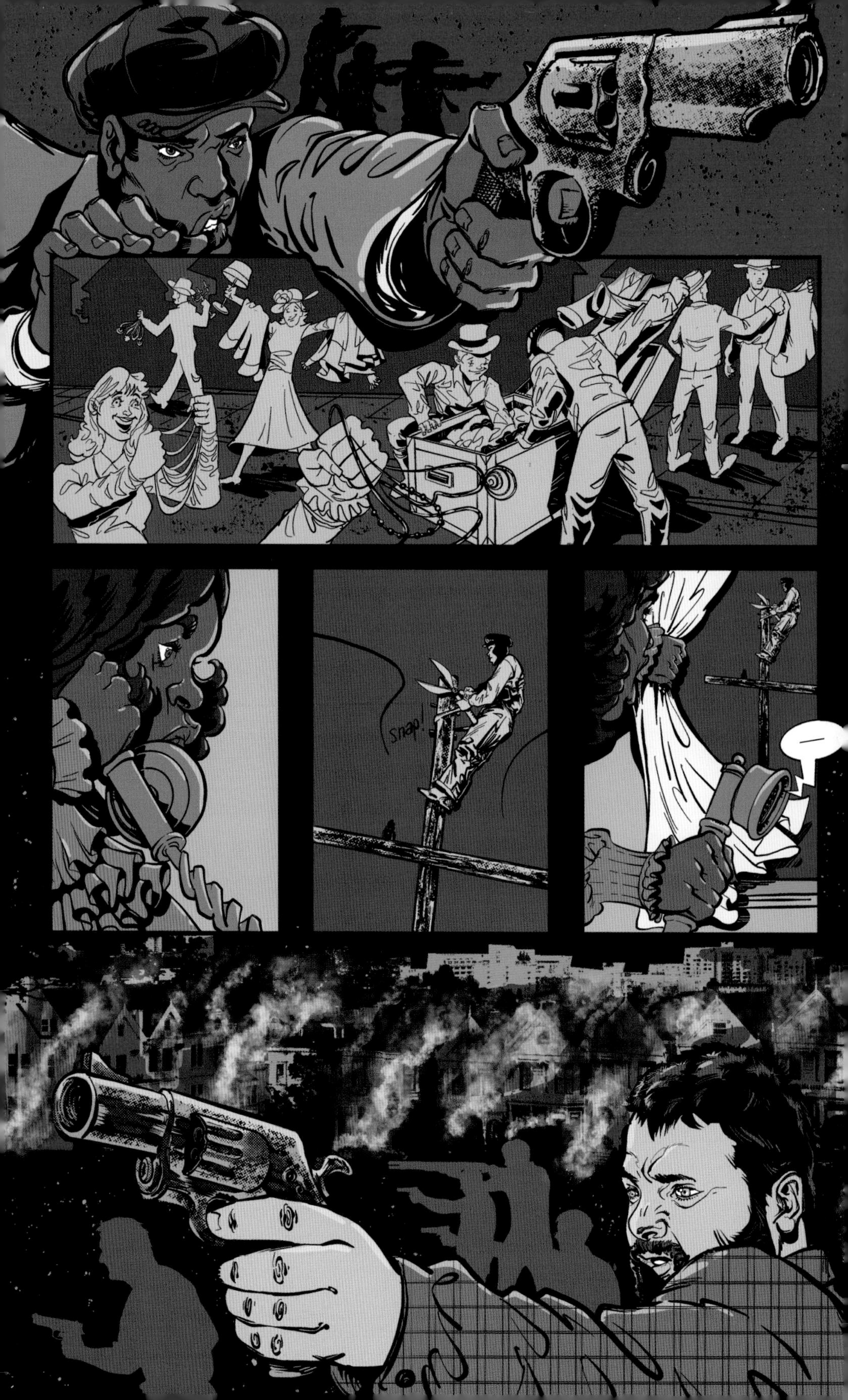
snap!
—

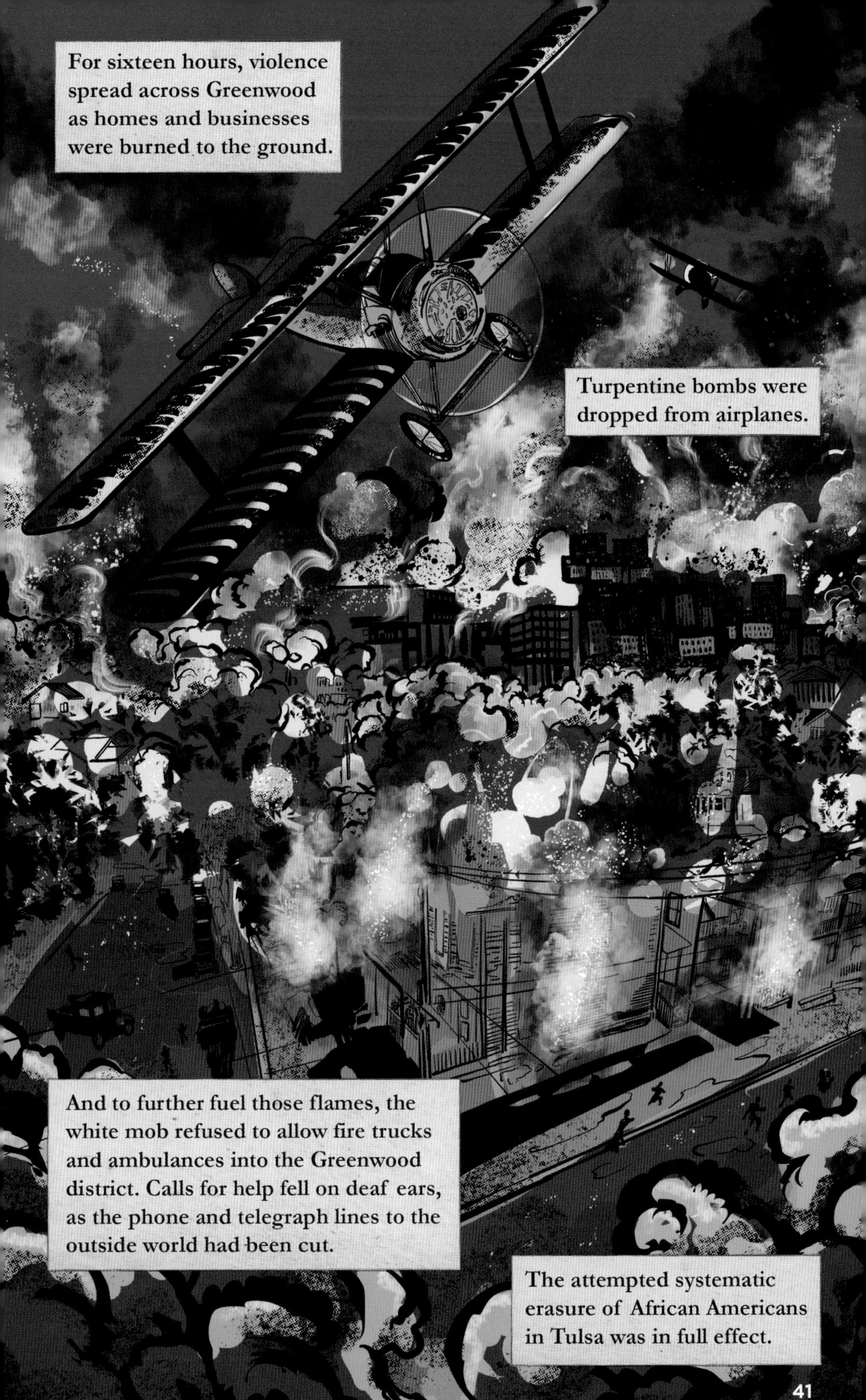
For sixteen hours, violence spread across Greenwood as homes and businesses were burned to the ground.
Turpentine bombs were dropped from airplanes.
And to further fuel those flames, the white mob refused to allow fire trucks and ambulances into the Greenwood district. Calls for help fell on deaf ears, as the phone and telegraph lines to the outside world had been cut.
The attempted systematic erasure of African Americans in Tulsa was in full effect.

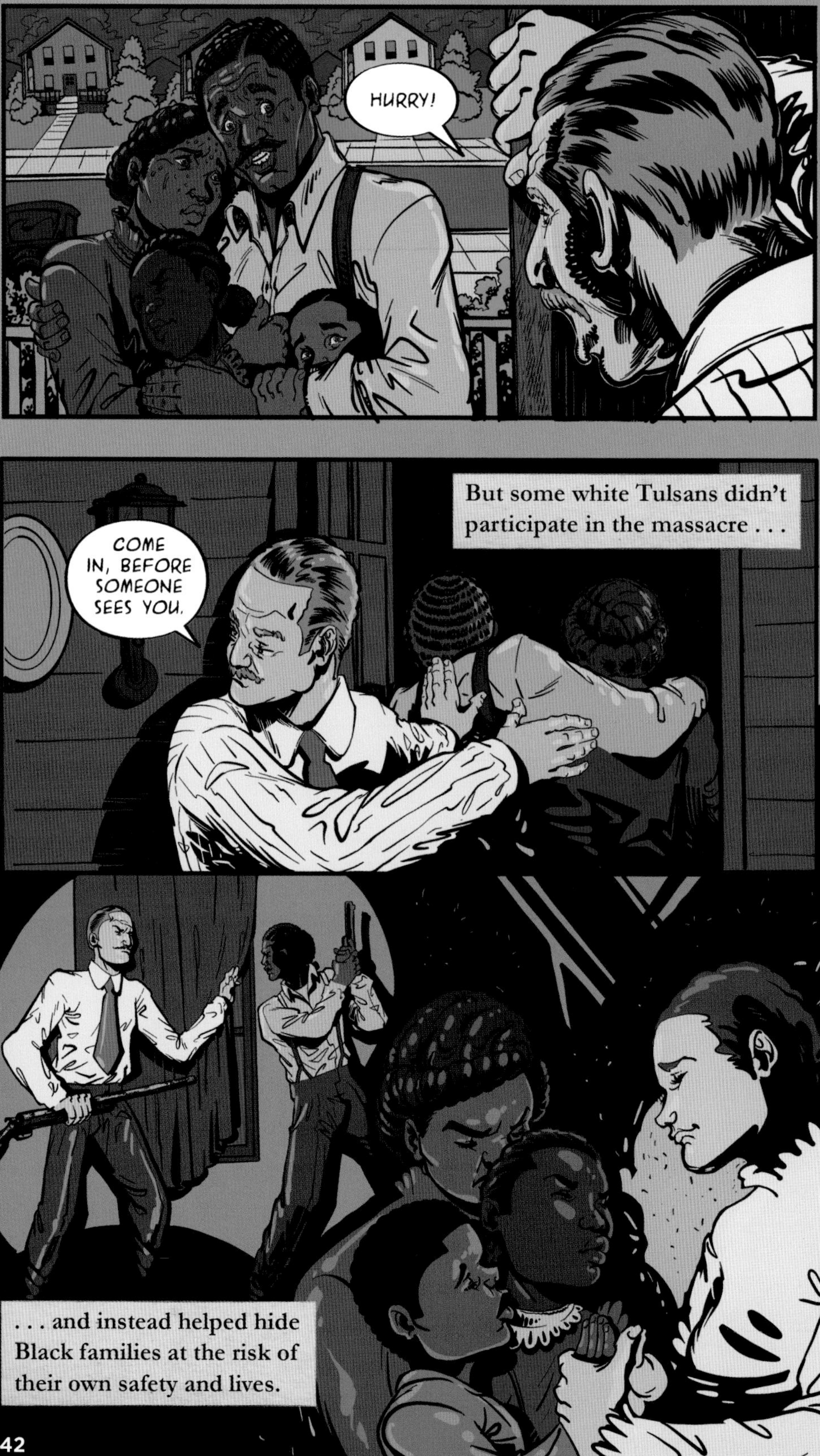
HURRY!
But some white Tulsans didn't participate in the massacre . . .
COME IN, BEFORE SOMEONE SEES YOU.
. . . and instead helped hide Black families at the risk of their own safety and lives.

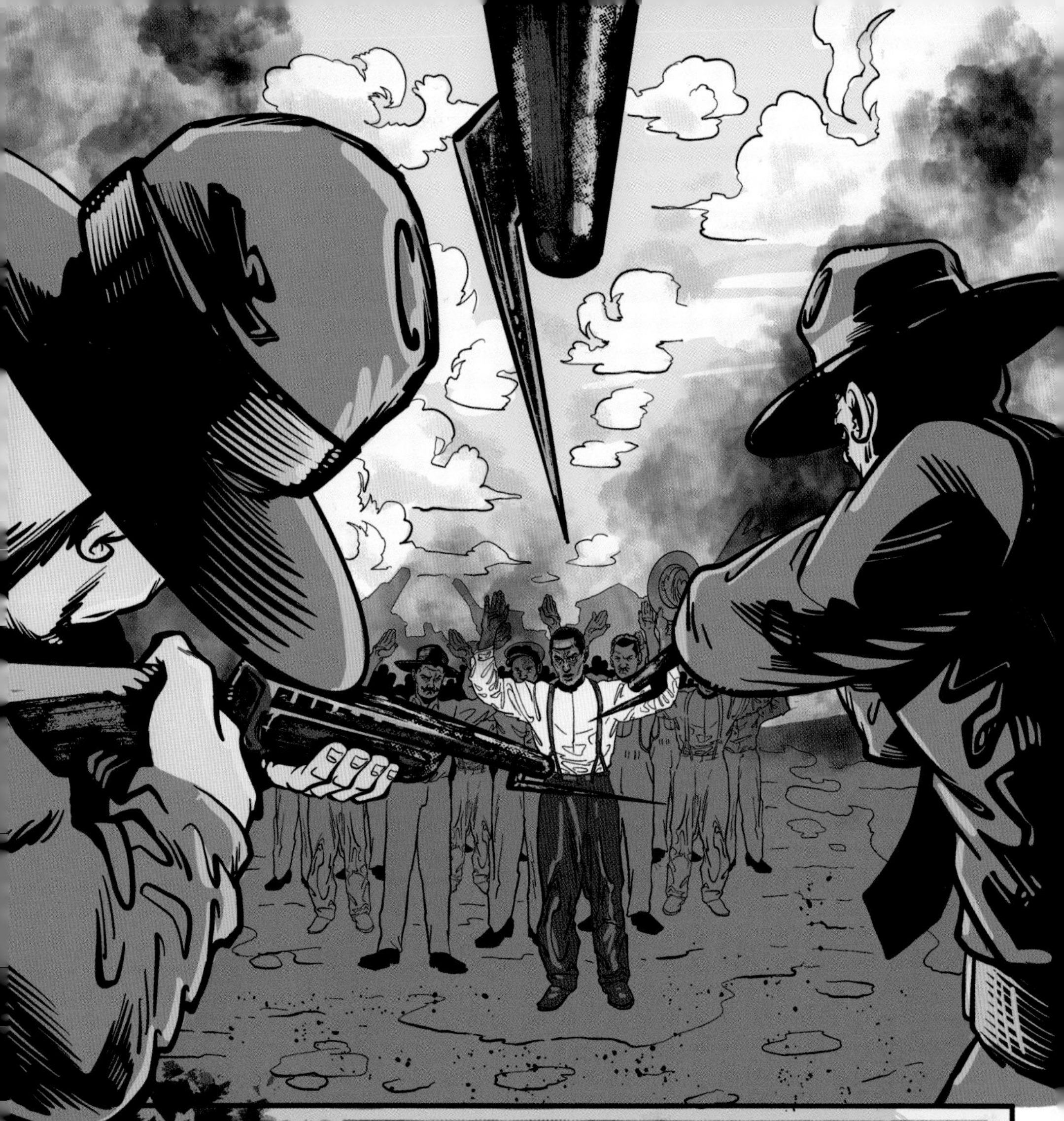

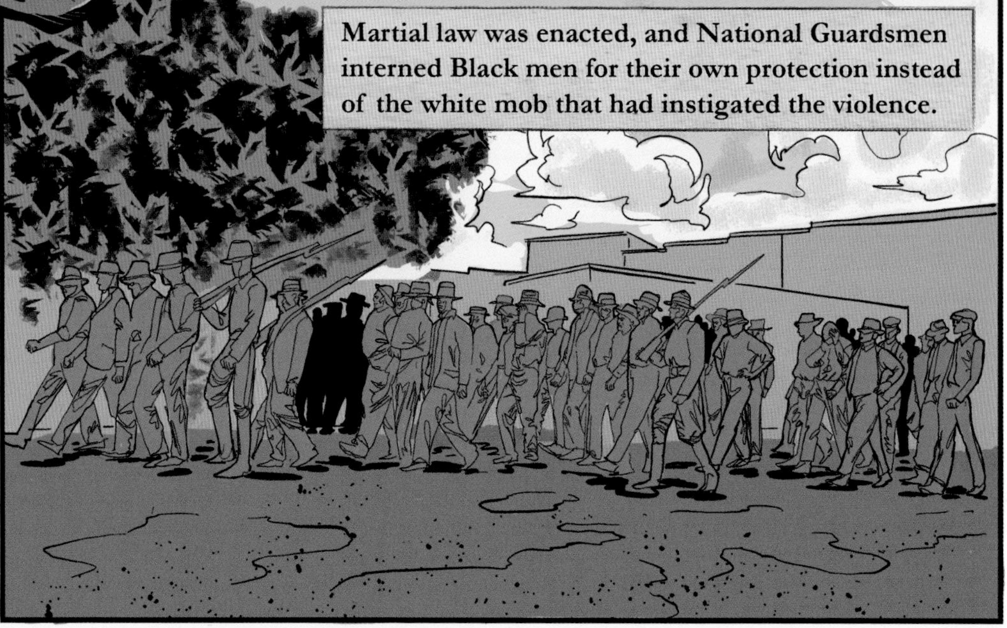
Martial law was enacted, and National Guardsmen interned Black men for their own protection instead of the white mob that had instigated the violence.

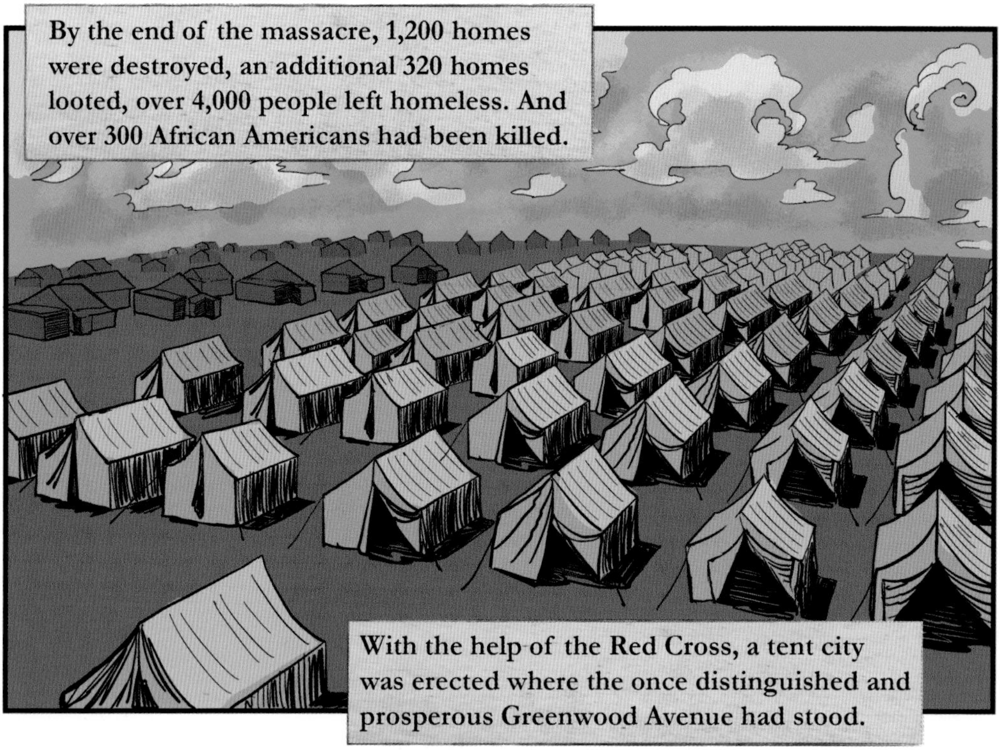
By the end of the massacre, 1,200 homes were destroyed, an additional 320 homes looted, over 4,000 people left homeless. And over 300 African Americans had been killed.
With the help of the Red Cross, a tent city was erected where the once distinguished and prosperous Greenwood Avenue had stood.

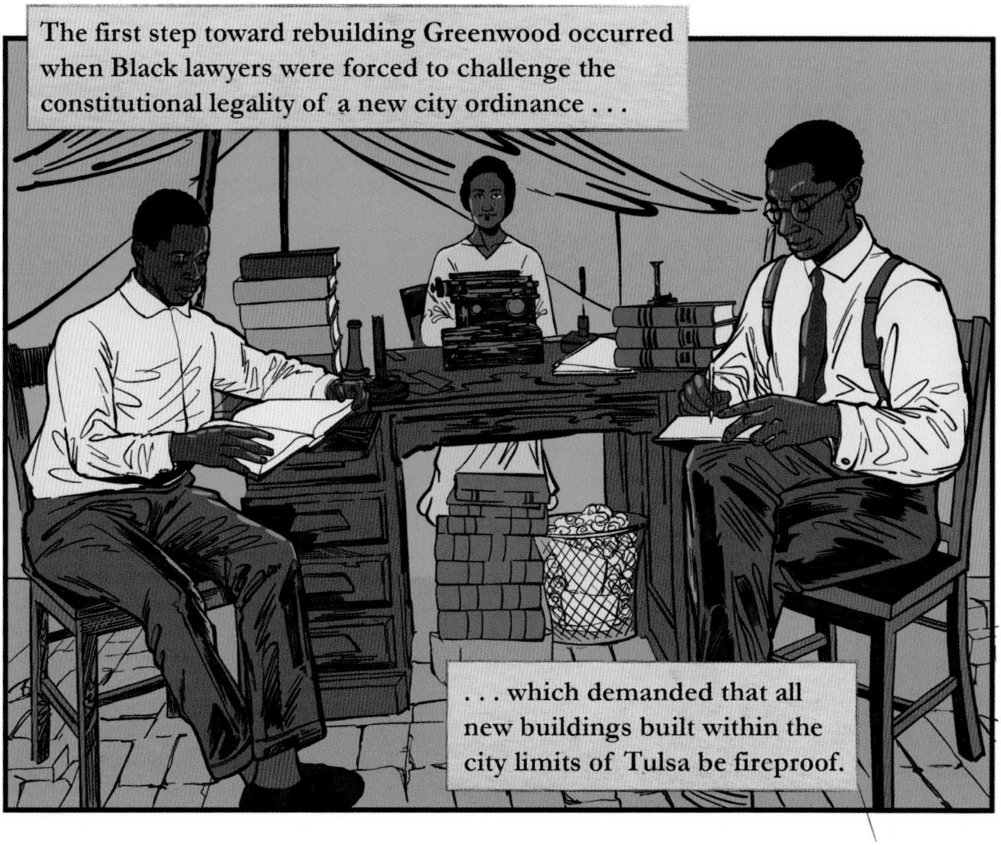
The first step toward rebuilding Greenwood occurred when Black lawyers were forced to challenge the constitutional legality of a new city ordinance . . .
. . . which demanded that all new buildings built within the city limits of Tulsa be fireproof.

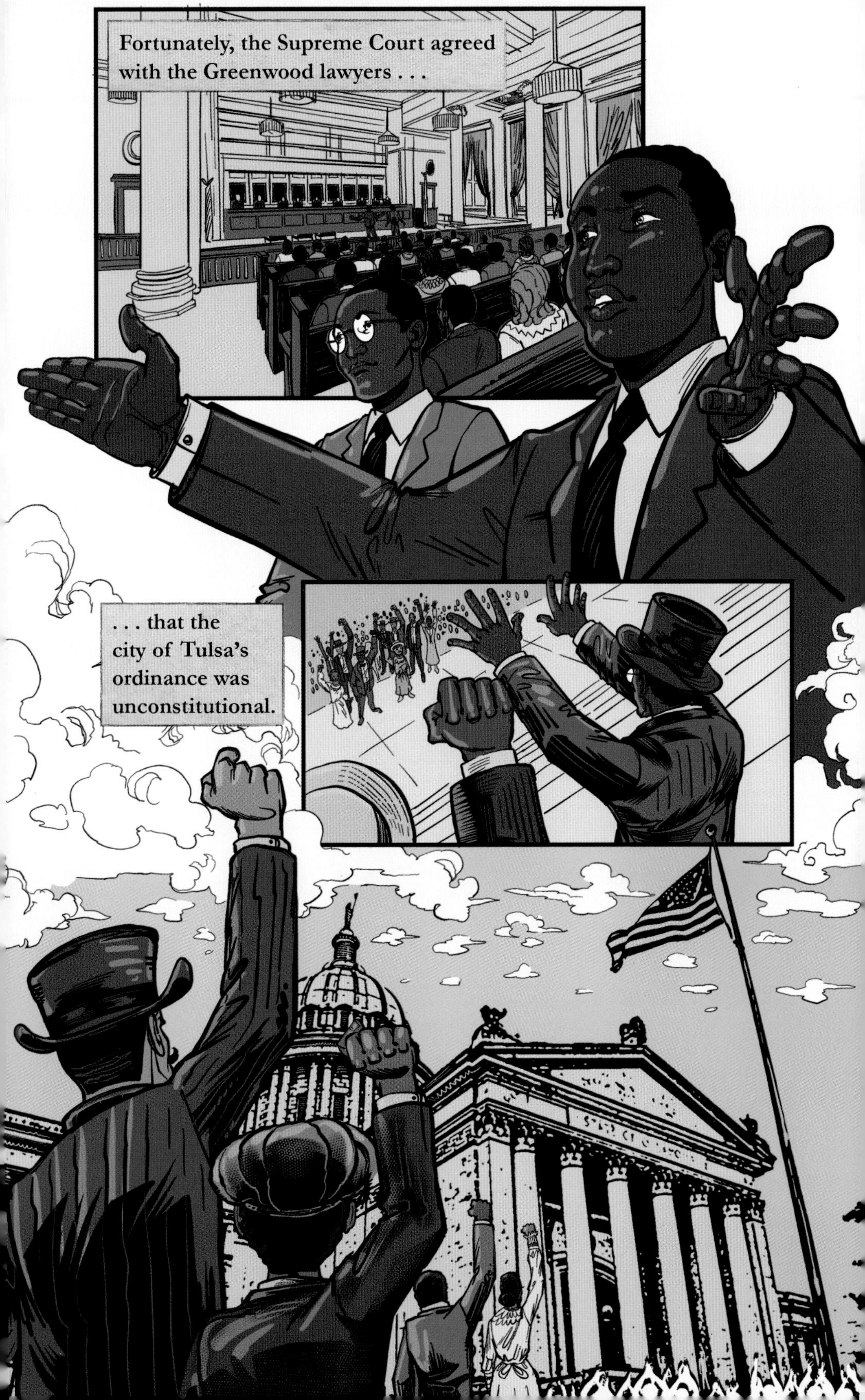
Fortunately, the Supreme Court agreed with the Greenwood lawyers . . .
. . . that the city of Tulsa's ordinance was unconstitutional.

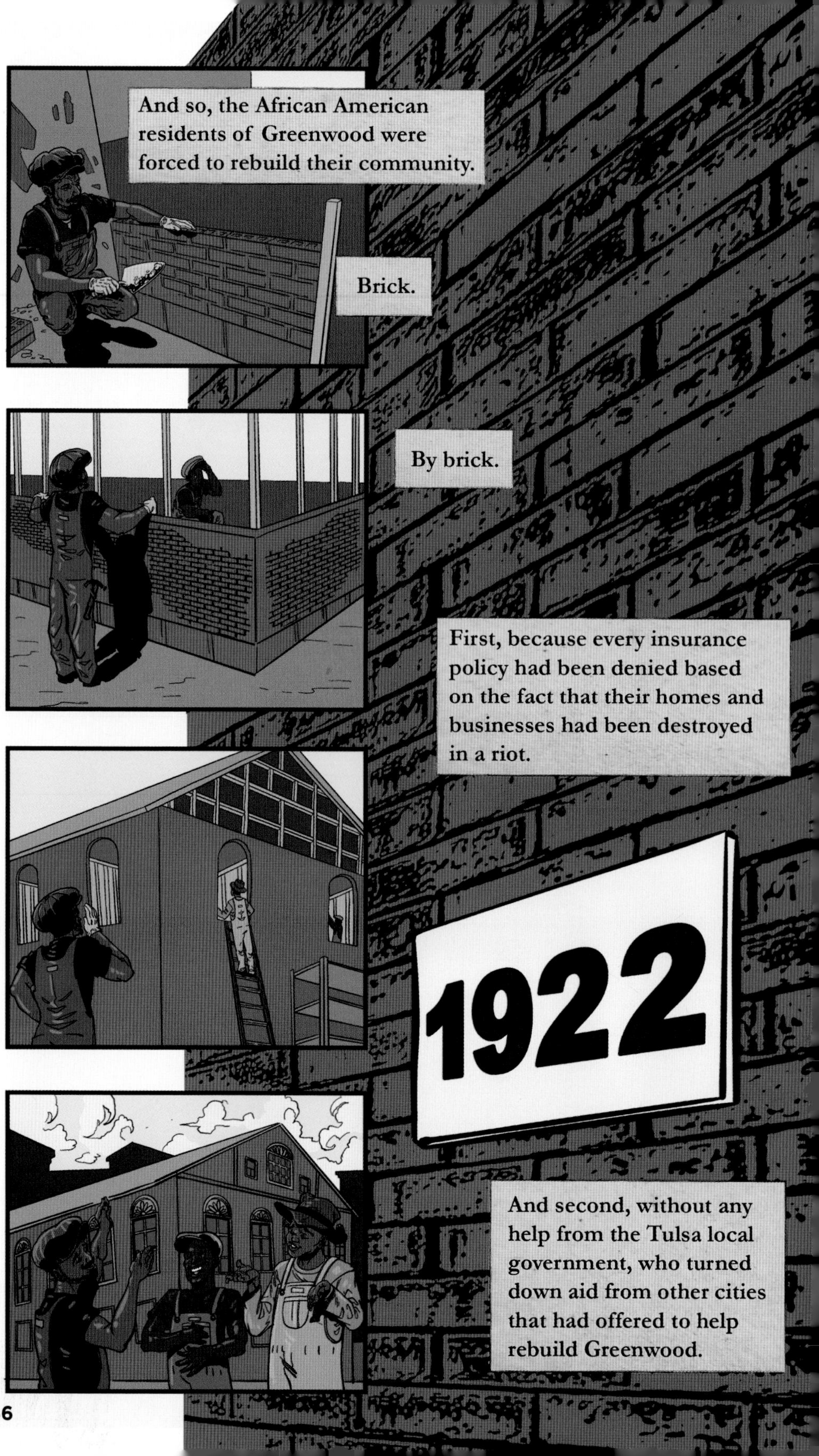
And so, the African American residents of Greenwood were forced to rebuild their community.
Brick.
By brick.
First, because every insurance policy had been denied based on the fact that their homes and businesses had been destroyed in a riot.
1922
And second, without any help from the Tulsa local government, who turned down aid from other cities that had offered to help rebuild Greenwood.

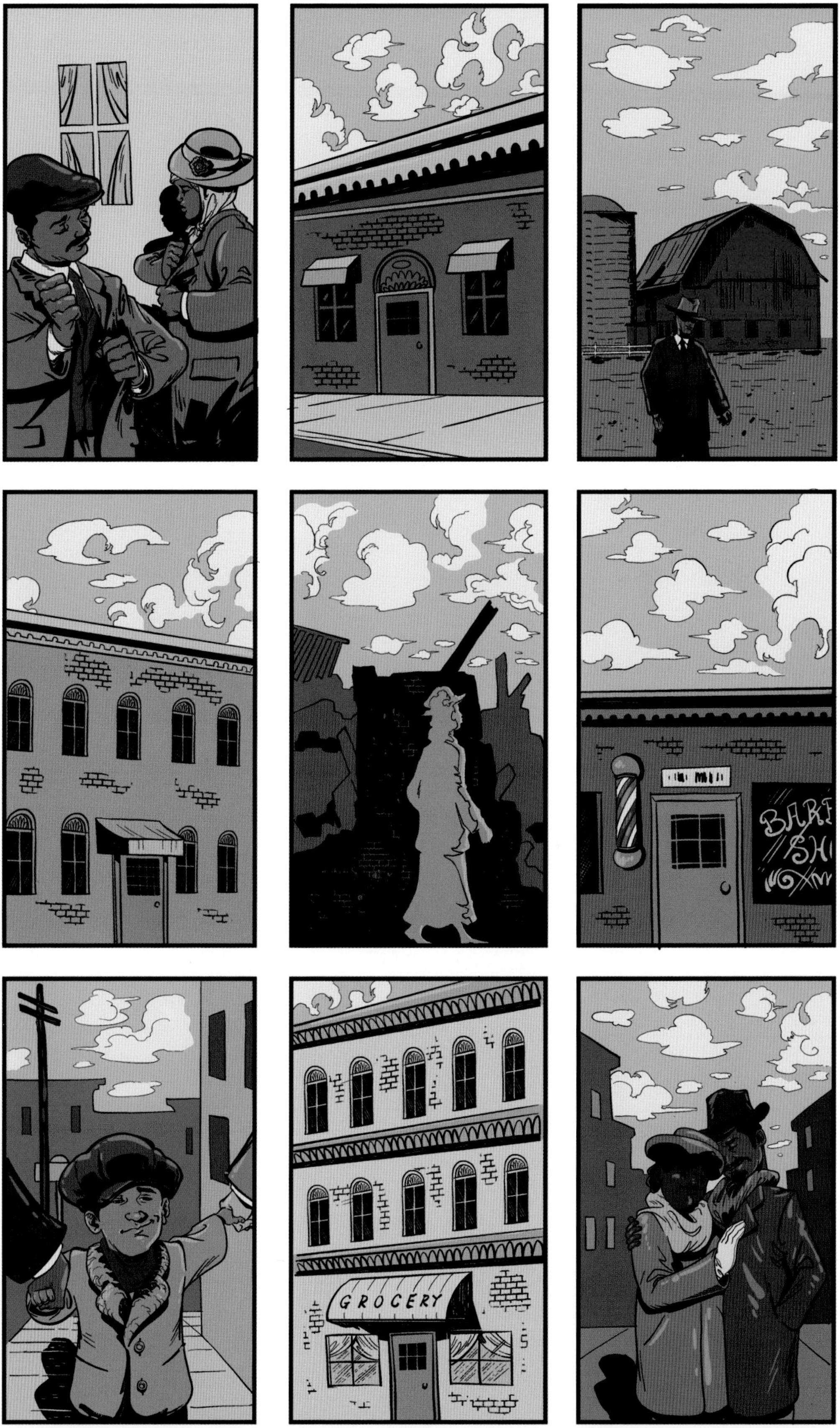
GROCERY

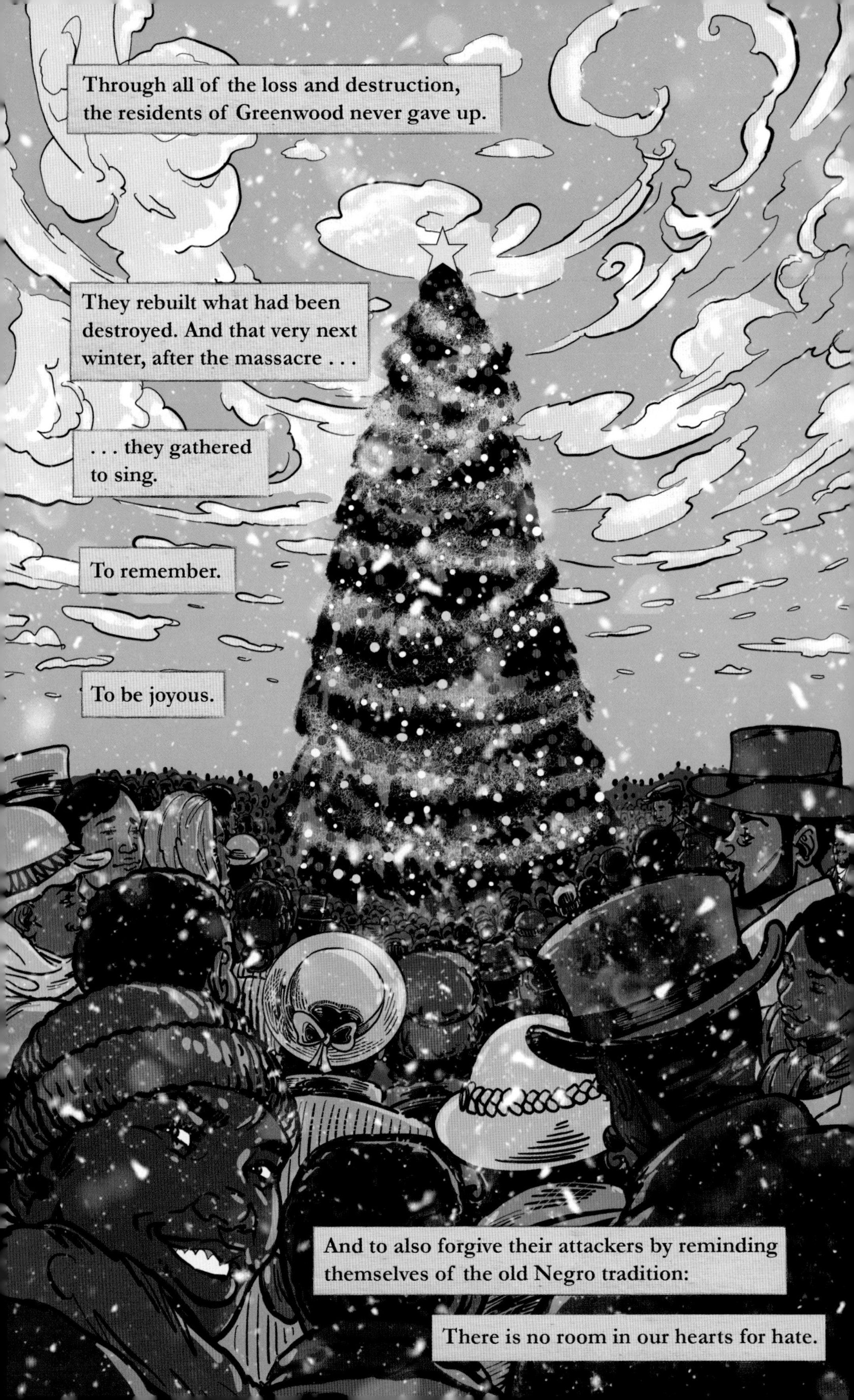
Through all of the loss and destruction, the residents of Greenwood never gave up.
They rebuilt what had been destroyed. And that very next winter, after the massacre . . .
. . . they gathered to sing.
To remember.
To be joyous.
And to also forgive their attackers by reminding themselves of the old Negro tradition:
There is no room in our hearts for hate.

IN SEARCH OF OUR FATHERS' GARDENS

Reynaldo Anderson, PhD • Dr. Colette Yellow Robe

The invasion and destruction of Black Wall Street in Tulsa, Oklahoma, in 1921 is a legacy of white supremacy and systematic racism in the United States toward people of African descent and American Indians. Although history records the event beginning with an altercation between an African American male named Dick Rowland and a white woman, Sarah Page, it was part of a pattern of racialized violence and genocide embedded in society. The environment and atmosphere surrounding the Tulsa "Black Wall Street" massacre was established during the earliest intrusions of Europeans onto the North American continent, American slavery and the Trail of Tears, and the Civil War and its aftermath during the Jim Crow era. The Oklahoma Territory became central to sanctioned violence and unchecked cessation of resources and lands of its American Indian and peoples of African descent populations. The Indigenous tribal nations to the Oklahoma Territory were forced to surrender lands by way of removal and withholding of provisions and rations from the U.S. government. As other tribal nations were forcibly removed to this territory as noted in the infamous Trail of Tears, the relocated tribes were subjected to land seizures and broken treaties. The tainted beginning of the Oklahoma Territory provided for a legal, social, and inevitable path to the horrid Tulsa Black Wall Street Massacre. The land itself was marked and stained with bloodshed, corruption, and a justification for the willful destruction of American Indians and African Americans.

Prior to the Oklahoma Territory, the Indigenous tribes were stewards of the land. There were long, tall prairie grasses that appeared like rolling waves in the winds. It was full of grazing animals like bison, which benefited from the rich vegetation. If you can imagine such a scene without the aid of technology, you will indeed see the natural state of the prairie without contamination from environmental disasters or plotted and parceled segments of land. Over time, the lands upon which Tulsa was built were home to the following Indigenous tribes: Kiikaapoi (Kickapoo), Wahzhazhe Maⁿzhaⁿ (Osage), Muscogee (Oklahoma), Caddo, Očhéthi Šakówiŋ (Lakota nations).[1]

The rapid spread of settlerism on the Great Plains brought forth a concerted agenda to further assimilate American Indian tribes and conquer the vast wilderness. A brutal tactic that was carried forward without any regard to the treaty negotiations or the peoples upon which modern civilization trampled. The Westward Expansion justified the encroachment of white colonists during the nineteenth century to advance an imperial agenda that dehumanized and set out to annihilate the original inhabitants of what would become the United States. Tribal nations were already moving from regions like the Ohio River valley area or the great Indigenous metropolis of St. Louis[2] to flee from the encroachment, and recorded by tribal oral histories. Eventually, the U.S. advanced its Westward Expansion plans with the extraction of tribes from Indigenous homelands and forced removal of tribes to the Oklahoma Territory. The Civil War and subsequent treaty signings, and the Dawes Act of 1887, were two significant points in history that did—and continues to do—grave harm to the tribes that were indigenous to Oklahoma and the relocated nations. It disrupted Native American tribes from their ways of knowing and roles as stewards to the land.

The legendary Standing Rock[3] Lakota author Vine Deloria Jr. captured the Western Agenda, which built upon the partnership and complicit actions between the U.S. government and Christian missionaries: "It has been said of missionaries that when they arrived they had only the Book, and we had the land; now we have the Book and they have the land." As Deloria Jr. noted, the key to Christianity's success was its ability to "differentiate life into segments" that were totally unrelated. As the Reformation successfully broke the world into two parts: church and state, this division utilized a form of moral justification for one another. The acts committed by the state that were immoral and endorsed by the church were to attain political power. Thus, the implementation of "uncivilized" acts of the government were made in partnership with the moral force in society, the church.

By the end of the 1880s, the U.S. Congress established a census record of the Five Civilized Tribes relocated in Oklahoma. This codification secured the de jure status of these tribal nations: Cherokees, Seminoles, Chickasaw, Creek, and Choctaws. Further, this is a prime example of how assimilation practices were elevated because these particular tribal nations chose to engage (willingly and unwillingly) in Western customs. As Deloria Jr. often iterated, the term "civilized" is a racist and colonial notion that directly implied that the tribal cultures were inferior. In fact, it is the subjectivity of the term that upholds colonialism, settlerism, and white supremacy.

After the seizures of lands and the opening of reservation lands through the Dawes Act, additional thefts of land and resources ensued. The early twentieth century revealed the seizure of mineral rights and resources in the Oklahoma Territory, soon to be a state. The Osage Nation, after removal from Kansas and western Missouri, were subjected to a planned and methodical campaign to usurp land and, most important, the mineral resources in the land. Yet the corruption that followed the oil reserves on their lands led to a brutal episode in their history. The Osage Nation remind us with their perspective on this dark period as they call it the "Reign of Terror."[4] The ramifications of these infamous murders among the Osage Nation are the flagrant reminder of tribal citizens treated as unintelligent, not entitled to the wealth from the oil profits, and the core racist tenet that the U.S. government must serve as the paternalizing agent for tribal peoples.

Finally, the simplistic notions that complexity, imagination, hybridity, and all forms of tribal organization and kinship system revolved around patriarchal notions is a mythical Western construct. Quecha scholar Sandy Grande[5] asserts that the influence and complex roles of women—not just for fertility—was prevalent among the vast tribal nations that encountered the very restrictive and limiting roles that Western society had for women in families and communities. The co-opting of the roles that Native American women have played in traditional Indigenous societies continues to plague the Western psyche as Pocahontas and Sacagawea litter the courtyards of several modern institutions of higher learning, and Native American women like Choctaw scholar Devon A. Mihesuah and Dakota scholar Angela Cavender Wilson have heralded the call for reform to inaccurate, racist, and unacceptable narratives.[6] It is critical to understand that Native American women held a respected status in most tribal nations and were able to inform powerful decision-making matters. Often, it was the Indigenous women who were consulted as the needs of tribes shifted and eventually encountered the encroachment of white settlerism on the Great Plains. The rigorous campaign to drive Native American tribes west or into exile was but one aspect of the way that Oklahoma became a convergence point in African Americans' and American Indians' extraordinary will to survive.

The African American presence was in Oklahoma in the early 1800s. Significant numbers of enslaved Africans and freedmen appeared in Oklahoma during the forced ethnic cleansing of American Indians during the Trail of Tears migration from 1828–36. For example, "African Creeks," or enslaved Africans owned by the Creek nation, were in the region when Muskogee was founded as a railroad town in 1872. African American freedmen and African Creeks formed the heart of a thriving African American community in eastern Oklahoma in the 1890s.

It was through this nexus of racial capitalism, American Indian nations, the federal government, and financial speculation that enslaved Africans had to fight, struggle, and transition into eventual citizenship. With approximately 4,600 enslaved Africans between them, the Cherokees were the largest property owners of enslaved Africans by 1860 at the onset of the American Civil War.[7] The Cherokee relied on these enslaved men and women as both interpreters and translators. However, these enslaved Africans worked on farms or as laborers and were under constant surveillance for fear of revolt, which eventually occurred in 1842 at Webbers Falls.

On November 15, 1842, twenty-five enslaved Africans from the Cherokee-owned Vann plantation revolted and locked up their owners and overseers in their homes. They stole supplies that included horses, ammunition, and food for a journey to Mexico, where slavery was illegal.

The militia caught up with the runaways near the area of the Red River on November 28, 1842. The incident provoked tension between free Black Seminoles and the Cherokee Nation, leading to the passage of a law requiring all free African Americans, except former Cherokee-enslaved Africans, to leave the proximity of the Cherokee Nation.

This conflict was characteristic of the tensions breaking out in the region leading up to the Civil War, with radicals like John Brown and others fighting over the issue of slavery. The Five Nations owned about ten thousand enslaved Africans at the onset of the Civil War in 1861. However, the system of slavery in the Five Nations was differentiated from the system of chattel slavery in the confederacy. For example, the Seminole and Creek often intermarried and allowed some range of freedom in contrast to the Cherokee, who did not intermarry with enslaved Africans, or the Chickasaw and Choctaw, who implemented systems that looked like Southern cotton plantations. Furthermore, enslaved Africans frequently were enculturated in the customs and social milieu of the Five Nations, and parts of the Territory were still a haven for runaways.

At the beginning of the Civil War, tensions emerged between the tribes over regional loyalty with the Union or the Confederacy, and over the issue of slavery. While some members of the Five Nations declared support for the Union, the majority from all the Indian nations in the Oklahoma Territory supported the Confederacy. Enslaved Africans were caught in the middle of this conflict as the war raged across Oklahoma and Kansas in a series of guerrilla war tactics. Following the conclusion of the Civil War, the Five Nations were punitively treated as members of the rebel faction that supported the Confederacy. Leaders of the Five Nations met in Arkansas and Washington, D.C., to deal with land concessions, the creation of a unified territorial government, the issue of railroads, and the status of the formerly enslaved Africans, or freedmen.

Each of the Five Nations dealt with separate treaties for the freedman during what was referred to as the Reconstruction era of the United States. For example, while the Seminole granted full rights to their freedmen, the Choctaw and Chickasaw were against adopting the freedman into their society on an equal status. Although the Choctaw granted rights by 1883, and the Cherokee by 1866, the Chickasaw never did. However, in the wake of these events, along with the Civil War and Reconstruction, Black nationalism, Pan-Africanism, and Black capitalism would be dominant strains of African American social and political practice in the Oklahoma Territory and state between 1890 and 1920.[8]

In the final decades of the century, during the rise of what is called the Jim Crow era, several local events would occur that strained relations between whites, the Five Nations, and the African American community. First, the General Allotment Act of 1887 created the Dawes Commission[9] and it actively interfered in the governance of the Five Nation commission and had the authority to do so with passage of the Curtis Act of 1898.[10] However, the opening of Indian land brought both Black and white settlers, as well as railroad and mining operations. Furthermore, while racial solidarity grew among African Americans, hostility from the Five Nations would grow under the influence of whites immigrating from the South to the Territory. Therefore, shortly after the Land Rush of 1889, it opened up the opportunity for settlement, and as many as fifty towns and communities arose where African Americans lived with self-governance during the Jim Crow era.

For example, following the end of Reconstruction and the beginning of the Jim Crow period of American life in the late nineteenth century, there was a spark in the African American community and civic life in response to the institutionalized racial oppression in what the historian Rayford Logan called the "nadir," or sense of hopelessness.[11] This spark influenced the growth of mutual aid societies, entrepreneurship, historically Black colleges, and Black social movements that reflected African resistance to the American institutional and social oppression of white supremacy. The Oklahoma Territory was uniquely situated at this historical moment of Jim Crow and imperialism, as it attracted a cross section of African Americans and Africans that saw an opportunity to establish a base of power that could protect and promote their interest in the context of a potential Black state.

In 1890, the *New York Times* reported the Oklahoma Territory was being promoted as the "New Mecca" or "Beulah Land" for African Americans.[12] The collapse of Reconstruction, Ku Klux Klan terrorism, and Black nationalism were part of the matrix that led to over fifty Black towns established in Oklahoma. For example, African American activist E. P. McCabe was one of the prominent leaders at the time who promoted Oklahoma as a potential Black state, and pressed President Benjamin Harrison for this opportunity, and the idea made it to the United States Congress.[13] McCabe was also a prominent influencer who helped get the historically Black institution Langston University established in the 1890s during a period marked by the *separate but equal* doctrine upheld by the U.S. Supreme Court in *Plessy v. Ferguson*. These sociopolitical events over a thirty-year period help set the stage for the Tulsa massacre.

BLACK WALL STREET

Despite the impact of Jim Crow laws and segregation, African Americans managed to develop thriving self-sustaining communities across the United States. Following the collapse of the Black state project, a white political faction successfully ejected African Americans from the political process and got Oklahoma established as a state in 1907. Nonetheless, the separate but equal doctrine allowed African Americans to practice capital development in their own segregated communities, and "Black Wall Street" became an important regional economic hub of Black economic power.[14] Greenwood, as it was called, was named by O. W. Gurley, an African American landowner from a town of the same name in Mississippi, who purchased the property in 1906.[15] Although Oklahoma had only two airports, several prominent Black families owned planes. The Vernon AME Church and the Black-owned barbershops and grocery stores, medical center, entertainment facilities, banking, and a diverse array of interests were emblematic of the racial uplift spirit of the community. The leadership of the community reflected the philosophy in W. E. B. Du Bois's book *The Souls of Black Folk*, and the concept of the Talented Tenth, or the best of the race preparing African Americans for the challenges of modern society.[16] Black Wall Street was part of a network of thriving communities that stretched from the Midwest through the South to the East Coast that nurtured African American creativity and expression in the early twentieth century and marked the coming of what the Harlem Renaissance philosopher Alain Locke would call the "New Negro."[17] The New Negro was the generation of African Americans born after the Civil War, who had not known the lash, and many served in World War I or the Spanish-American War. The Greenwood area successfully survived the Spanish flu pandemic of 1918 that was brought home from World War I by American troops, as well as the racial terror of the Red Summer of 1919. However, it would not survive the vicious white supremacist violence of the spring of 1921.

On May 31, 1921, a young Black man named Dick Rowland was accused of assaulting a white woman, and an angry mob of whites gathered and attempted to lynch him, but a group of African Americans resisted. Tension already existed between white police officers and the African American community over their regular abuse of Black citizens. The stage for a massacre was set. With white law enforcement calling in for military assistance, north Tulsa became the first American community to be bombed from the air, and in the subsequent carnage, up to three hundred people were killed and thousands made homeless. North Tulsa was not alone in its experience of massacre and burning, as African American communities like Rosewood in Florida and East St. Louis in Illinois were among the towns destroyed during this period.

Following the destruction of Black Wall Street, it was slowly rebuilt by the 1940s, as some African American residents returned and attempted to revive their prospects. However, after WWII, as integration slowly took hold, it never regained the vitality it had enjoyed in previous decades.[18] In recent decades, there has finally been an attempt to acknowledge the destruction and suffering of the event of the time as several commissions and information has become more widely available, and survivors were able to share their stories. Yet the Tulsa massacre remains a cautionary tale of how systemic racism has been used to inflict destruction and suffering on Indigenous and minority communities in the United States. In modern times, the landmark case *McGirt v. Oklahoma*[19] and its subsequent decision by the United States Supreme Court in 2020, ruled that the eastern part of the state remains as Native American lands. A modern-day victory for the rights of Native American tribes, which provides inroads for new narratives of justice and change. Thus, our fathers' gardens reveal the stories of strength, resolve, and actualizing the impossible that can guide us into the future.

ABOUT THE ESSAY AUTHORS

Dr. Colette M. Yellow Robe's cultural and familial background inspires her to create authentic strategies in education and leadership. As an enrolled citizen of the Northern Cheyenne Tribe in Montana who grew up on the Winnebago Reservation in Nebraska, she advocates and implements concrete changes in Native communities to support diversity, inclusivity, and anti-racism and uphold tribal rights and sovereignty.

Reynaldo Anderson, PhD, currently serves as associate professor of communication studies at Harris-Stowe State University in Saint Louis, Missouri. Anderson is currently the executive director and co-founder of the Black Speculative Arts Movement (BSAM), an international network of artists, intellectuals, creatives, and activists. He is the co-editor of the anthologies and journals: *Afrofuturism 2.0: The Rise of Astro-Blackness* and *Cosmic Underground: A Grimoire of Black Speculative Discontent*, among others.

ENDNOTES

1   Native Land Digital, 2018, accessed September 2020, https://native-land.ca.

2   Charles Mann, *1491: New Revelations of the Americas Before Columbus* (New York: Vintage, 2011).

3   Vine Deloria Jr., *Custer Died for Your Sins: An Indian Manifesto* (Norman, OK: University of Oklahoma Press, 1988).

4   David Grann, *Killers of the Flower Moon: The Osage Murders and the Birth of the FBI* (New York: Doubleday, 2017).

5   Sandy Grande, *Red Pedagogy: Native American Social and Political Thought* (Lanham, MD: Rowan and Littlefield, 2004).

6   Devon A. Mihesuah and Angela Cavender Wilson, *Indigenizing the Academy: Transforming Scholarship and Empowering Communities* (Lincoln: University of Nebraska Press, 2004).

7   Barbara Krauthamer, "Slavery," *The Encyclopedia of Oklahoma History and Culture*, https://www.okhistory.org/publications/enc/entry.php?entry=SL003.

8   Jeremiah Wilson Moses, *The Golden Age of Black Nationalism: 1850–1925* (New York: Oxford University Press, 1988).

9   Armen H. Merjian, "An Unbroken Chain of Injustice: The Dawes Act, Native American Trusts, and Cobell v. Salazar," *Gonzaga Law Review* 46, no. 3 (2010).

10 Merjian, "An Unbroken Chain of Injustice."

11 Rayford Whittingham Logan, *The Negro in American life and thought: The Nadir, 1877–1901* (New York: Dial Press, 1954).

12 Julie Bisbee, "How Oklahoma Almost Became a Black State," *The Oklahoman*, February 29, 2008, oklahoman.com/article/3210110/how-oklahoma-almost-became -a-black-state.

13 Jere Roberson, "McCabe, Edward P.," *The Encyclopedia of Oklahoma History and Culture*, https://www.okhistory.org/publications/enc/entry.php?entry=MC006.

14 Moses, *The Golden Age of Black Nationalism.*

15 Kimberly Fain, "The Devastation of Black Wall Street," *JSTOR Daily*, July 5, 2017, https://daily.jstor.org/the-devastation-of-black-wall-street/.

16 W. E. B. Du Bois, *The Souls of Black Folk* (New York: Oxford University Press, 2008).

17 Alain Locke, *The New Negro* (New York: Arno, 1968).

18 Fain, "The Devastation of Black Wall Street."

19 *McGirt v. Oklahoma*, 591 U.S. (2020), https://www.supremecourt.gov /opinions/19pdf/18-9526_9okb.pdf.

Barmore, Jasmin. "Campaign to rebuild Black Wall Street could extend to Detroit." *The Detroit News*. June 18, 2020. www.detroitnews.com/story/news/local/detroit -city/2020/06/18/campaign-rebuild-black-wall-street-could-extend-detroit/3214278001.

Bisbee, Julia. "How Oklahoma almost became a black state." *The Oklahoman*. February 29, 2008. http://oklahoman.com/article/3210110/how-oklahoma-almost-became-a-black-state.

"Choctaw (Chahta')," Omniglot, https://www.omniglot.com/writing/choctaw.htm.

Deloria, Jr., Vine. *Custer Died for Your Sins: An Indian Manifesto*. Norman: University of Oklahoma Press, 1988.

Du Bois, W.E.B. *The Souls of Black Folk*. New York: Oxford University Press, 2008.

Duncan, Graham A. "Ethiopianism in Pan-African Perspective, 1880–1920." *Studia Historiae Ecclesiasticae* 41, no. 2 (2015): 198–218.

Fain, Kimberly. "The Devastation of Black Wall Street." *JSTOR Daily*. July 5, 2017.

Grande, Sandy. *Red Pedagogy: Native American Social and Political Thought*. Lanham, MD: Rowan and Littlefield Publishers, 2004.

Grann, David. *Killers of the Flower Moon: The Osage Murders and the Birth of the FBI*. New York: Doubleday, 2017.

Kauunui, J. Kēhaulani, ed. *Speaking of Indigenous Politics: Conversations with Activists, Scholars, and Tribal Leaders*. Minneapolis: University of Minnesota Press, 2018.

Krauthamer, Barbara. "Slavery." *The Encyclopedia of Oklahoma History and Culture*. https:// www.okhistory.org/publications/enc/entry.php?entry=SL003.

Locke, Alain, ed. *The New Negro: An Interpretation*. New York: Arno Press and the New York Times, 1968.

Logan, Rayford Whittingham. *The Negro in American Life and Thought: The Nadir, 1877– 1901*. New York: Dial Press, 1954.

Mann, Charles C. *1491: New Revelations of the Americas Before Columbus*. New York: Vintage, 2011.

McGirt v. Oklahoma. 591 U.S. (2020) www.supremecourt.gov/opinions/19pdf/18 -9526_9okb.pdf.

Merjian, Armen H. "An Unbroken Chain of Injustice: The Dawes Act, Native American Trusts, and Cobell v. Salazar." *Gonzaga Law Review* 46, no. 3 (2010): 609.

Mihesuah, Devon Abbott, and Angela Cavender Wilson, eds. *Indigenizing the Academy: Transforming Scholarship and Empowering Communities*. Lincoln, NE: Bison Books, 2004.

Moore, Moses N. 1986. *Orishatukeh Faduma: Liberal Theology and Evangelical Pan-Africanism, 1857–1946*. Lanham, MD: Rowman & Littlefield Publishers, 1996.

Moses, Wilson Jeremiah. *The Golden Age of Black Nationalism, 1850–1925*. New York: Oxford University Press, 1988.

Native Land Digital, 2018, accessed September 2020, http://native-land.ca.

O'Dell, Larry. "Chief Alfred Sam." *The Encyclopedia of Oklahoma History and Culture*. www.okhistory.org/publications/enc/entry.php?entry=CH040.

Roberson, Jere. "McCabe, Edward P." *The Encyclopedia of Oklahoma History and Culture*. www.okhistory.org/publications/enc/entry.php?entry=MC006.

ACKNOWLEDGMENTS

I'd like to thank God for blessing me with the talent to see story like Ray Charles heard music. I'd also like to thank Chakira Lane for her support. I'd like to thank John Jennings and all the staff at Abrams ComicArts/Megascope. Lastly, I'd like to remember and thank the citizens of Greenwood, past and present, because without your voices rising through the depths of history, none of this would have been possible.

—*Alverne Ball*

I'd like to thank Alverne Ball for trusting me with his vision. My children, Solomon and Nyla, who inspire me to use the rest of my life to build a better world for their descendants to inherit. Special thanks to Motherboxx Studios, the Black Speculative Arts Movement, "Skip" Gates, Marcyliena Morgan, Cornel West, Bakari Kitwana, and my family at the Hutchins Center for African & African American Research. Also, many thanks to Abrams Books for allowing space for Megascope and for recognizing the importance and sensitivity of this project. This is what allyship looks like. I honor the perseverance of Black people who boldly do more than survive by defiantly living. Who awaken from their nightmares and at night, dare to dream again. Who from generations past sacrificed those same dreams so that we, in this ultimate time of ours, would operate in our highest gifts, goals, and aspirations for a tomorrow people. We are in this great moment standing on the mountaintop overlooking the promised land created through speculative philosophies, theories, technologies, and arts, all from our greatest imaginings—and promise—to utilize our power by understanding our great responsibility to actualize the world our ancestors did not live to see. We are truly our ancestor's wildest dreams.

—*Stacey Robinson*

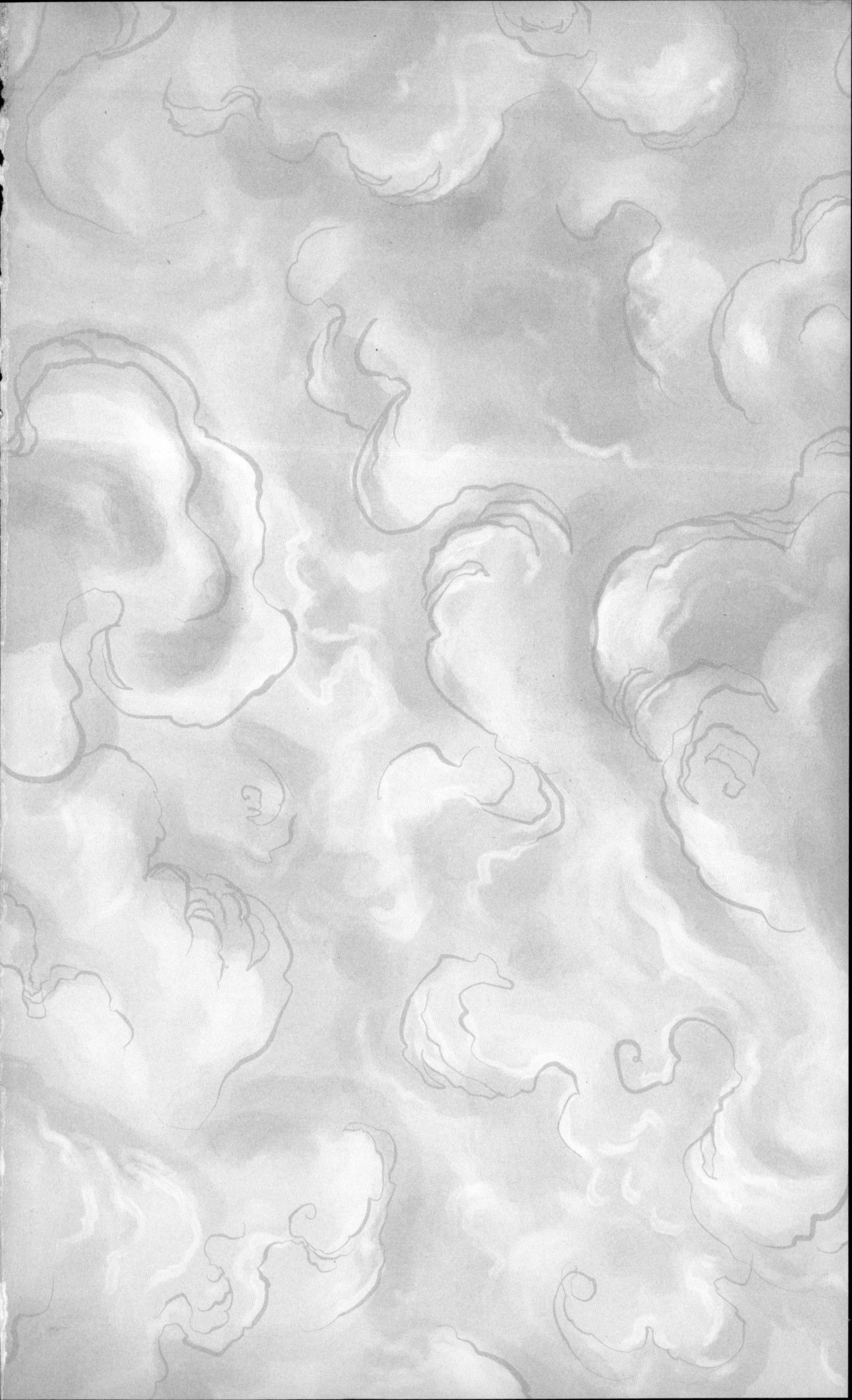